The Future
of Protestant Worship:
Beyond the Worship Wars

Ronald P. Byars

Westminster John Knox Press
LOUISVILLE • LONDON

Scripture quotations, unless otherwise indicated, are from the New Revised Standard Version of the Bible, copyright © 1989 by the Division of Christian Education of the National Council of the Churches of Christ in the U.S.A., and are used by permission.

Book design by Sharon Adams
Cover design by Jennifer K. Cox
Cover photograph: © Hans Neleman/Allsport/Getty Images

First edition
Publised by Westminster John Knox Press
Louisville, Kentucky

This book is printed on acid-free paper that meets the American National Standards Institute Z39.48 standard. ♾

PRINTED IN THE UNITED STATES OF AMERICA

03 04 05 06 07 08 09 10 11 — 10 9 8 7 6 5 4 3

Library of Congress Cataloging-in-Publication Data

Byars, Ronald P.
   The future of Protestant worship : beyond the worship wars / Ronald P. Byars.
      p. cm.
   Includes bibliographical references (p.).
   ISBN 0-664-22572-1 (alk. paper)
   1. Public worship.   2. Protestant churches—Doctrines.
I. Title.

BV15 .B93 2002
264—dc21

2002023005

For Steve and Lisa
Matt and Melissa
Jonas, Grace, Audrey, and Benjamin

Contents

Introduction

We live in an entrepreneurial age. With the demise of the Marxist economies, the free market has apparently triumphed, and with the free market comes the entrepreneur. The growth of the Internet has spurred many an ambitious graduate to dream of starting an electronically based business of her or his own rather than going to work for an existing corporation. Being one's own boss is within the range of possibilities for those with imagination and determination. The fact that only a few will succeed to the degree that they expect doesn't seem to serve as a deterrent. Throughout the marketplace, the courageous and those with nothing to lose are striking out in new directions.

The spirit of the entrepreneur is alive and well in the church too. The late twentieth century witnessed the tremendous successes of religious experiments led by a few with a pioneering mentality. The influence of Robert Schuller's Crystal Cathedral encouraged Bill Hybels

1

and his associates to launch a new venture, which became the Willow Creek Community Church in South Barrington, Illinois. Many apprentices have created clones of that church, some members of the Willow Creek Association, others not. Other pioneers, such as Chuck Smith, Ken Gulliksen, John Wimber, and Ralph Moore, have created churches specifically designed for a new generation, such as Calvary Chapel, the Vineyard churches, and Hope Chapel.[1] Many other entrepreneurs, perhaps drawing their inspiration from one or another of these models, have created congregations that worship in nontraditional ways, and often draw large crowds of baby boomers and Gen-Xers. At the same time, many pastors in traditional congregations, taking courage from these examples, have dared to create new alternative services or to introduce changes into existing ones.

WHY CHANGE?

What, other than a pioneering spirit, drives these changes? In some cases, it seems to be a passion for evangelism, and particularly for reaching out to generations largely missing from traditional churches. In other cases, it seems to be an attempt to hold on to church members who are bored and reluctant worshipers. Sometimes, it may be an attempt to duplicate the fabulous numerical successes of single-generation congregations. But behind these various motivating factors, there is the inescapable fact of dramatic cultural change. What used to work just fine (or seemed to) doesn't work anymore.

It seems as though society has broken into pieces. What do people want? What would nourish their spirits? How might the church structure its worship to speak to people's spiritual hunger? Apparently, even those who think they know the answers to such questions find that neither the questions nor the answers precisely fit everybody. If there ever was a typical American, there is no longer. Even those who manage to draw large crowds to their services don't appeal to everyone even in the same generational cohort. But it seems evident that what used to meet worshipers' expectations has lost its attractiveness for many. Worship that suited people in the 1950s draws fewer and fewer, while the bold experiments have a reputation for numerical success. Everybody prefers the big numbers, but there are problems with designing worship by taking a poll.

There is much to admire in the spirit of those who take risks for the sake of the gospel. At the same time, risk-taking is more than just impulsively charging in new directions. Jesus speculated about the likely fortunes of a king who rushes into a conflict with a neighboring monarch, imagining, no doubt, great rewards in victory. However, the king hadn't seriously considered the costs of this venture (Luke 14:31). Wisdom requires clear thinking, whatever the project. Those who pioneer in worship will want to consider whether worship is meant to be a tool for evangelism and/or recruitment of new members, and if so, whether those are its primary purposes. They will want to ask what happens when worship is bent to serve an evangelism and recruitment agenda, and whether the costs are worth it.

WHAT'S AT STAKE?

Is anything really essential to Christian worship? Or is worship simply a blank page, an empty hour or so to be filled with whatever seems religious? Is it possible to worship in the idiom of popular culture without oversimplifying and even distorting the gospel? Or, by turning its back on contemporary cultural forms, does the church become elitist, inaccessible to large numbers of people? Should these questions even be addressed without at least some minimal consultation with Scripture, theology, and history, as well as sociology? Interested parties have answered all these questions differently. Since a great deal is at stake, it's no surprise that passions rise when dealing with them. No doubt that's why some have come to speak of "worship wars."

It's in this environment that we see more and more churches describing their services as "traditional" or "contemporary." I suspect that in more cases than not, the differences are superficial. The music will almost certainly be different. But very often, the presuppositions behind so-called contemporary worship are not significantly different from those behind so-called traditional worship. However great the differences in style, both proceed from the same worldview, shaped by the common culture. Superficial differences between traditional and contemporary will certainly seem momentous to those accustomed to one or the other, but they may very well be only variations on a single theme. For mainline churches, these changes are often equivalent to rearranging the deck chairs on the Titanic.

It's clear to many stakeholders that the worship of mainline Protestants is in need of reform. What's not so clear is what shape that reform ought to take. Pioneers who have ventured into new territories have helped to show us what the issues are. Certainly they have alerted us to the inescapable fact that many in our society have not felt nourished by the worship that apparently suited their parents. The worship entrepreneurs show us both the possibilities and the land mines that become evident when we introduce change in worship. How do we sift the learnings available from those who have led the charge? What yardsticks do we use to measure the value of particular efforts? And should we not also use the same standards to evaluate those services so often described as traditional?

There's a greeting-card type of sentiment that wishes for our children both wings and roots. With wings, they fly off to new ventures; with roots, they plant themselves firmly in valued relationships and proven virtues. Those who love the church might wish that its worship would show evidence that the people of God have both wings and roots. Christian worship has been constantly shifting, developing, in motion for as long as there is any historical record. It will certainly continue to change, to blow where the Spirit blows, we hope, or perhaps to be blown about by every wind of doctrine (Eph. 4:14)! But though Christian worship is on the wing, it cannot be truly Christian if it doesn't also have roots. We are, unavoidably, an historical people. We are rooted in the Scriptures, both the Hebrew Scriptures and the Scriptures of the new covenant. That history has a claim on us. That same history has instructed and shaped, to one degree or another, countless generations that have been similarly rooted in it. No matter how contemporary we are, we are members, as the Apostles' Creed says, of a "holy catholic church" and a "communion of saints." The church needs to be mindful of its roots for fear of cutting off a basic source of nourishment. While we need to be attentive to the moment, tuned in to the historical epoch and the particular culture in which we live, we also need to keep an ear open to the experience of the whole church, which includes generations gone before us.

My academic training has been in history, and my mind tends to work in historical ways. How did things get to be the way they are? What influences have shaped the church's movement in one direction rather than in some other? Judging from where we started out, is where we are where we need to be? The habit of looking at things from an historical point of view also shapes a way of looking at what's happening now. Can we discern what forces are at work in society and pressing upon the church? How do changes in society change the people within that society? How can the church, particularly in its worship, relate to people who are both similar to and different from people who have lived in other times?

THE USE-LESSNESS OF WORSHIP

While I try to address some of these questions, it will become clear that I am not without my own commitments. I am persuaded that while worship may have an evangelistic dimension, it's not primarily about evangelizing people or recruiting new members. In fact, when it's at its best, worship is and ought to be use-less. In other words, worship is not meant to serve some practical purpose, even though in fact it does serve many practical purposes. Recent newspaper articles tell of objective studies which show that people who worship regularly are likely to heal faster and live longer. That would seem to promise a very practical use for worship! However, I suspect that anyone who would read about such studies, and choose to go to church every Sunday just to share in those benefits, isn't likely to profit from the experiment. Worship isn't a means to an end; it's an end in itself.

I am further persuaded that how we spend our time in the Sunday assembly isn't an entirely open option, but that God has provided us with certain means which we ignore to our peril. To use traditional language, the means with which God has provided us are Word and sacrament. Both are deeply rooted in Scripture, and their value has been attested over and over from the first centuries of the Christian Era onward. Indeed, not infrequently their value has become evident from the harm caused when one or another has been marginalized or distorted.

It was only a few years ago that pundits were celebrating the success of the Japanese economy and bemoaning the end of American dominance. Or that some were celebrating the rise of the New South and predicting the near-abandonment of the so-called Rust Belt, the northern industrial cities. In just a few years, the prognoses of the futurists have been proven embarrassingly wrong! There is more than one historical example of religious movements that have stirred a lot of passion, drawn a significant constituency, and then lost their steam. Some of today's dwindling denominations once seemed to be the wave of the future. On the other hand, some of the religious movements that were nearly invisible to mainstream society fifty years ago now attract the children and grandchildren of those who once scorned them. Time has a way of altering the social and religious landscape.

THE RISKS OF PROGNOSTICATION

There is a certain risk, then, in tying one's fortunes too closely to contemporary trends. It would be foolhardy to try to predict the future of worship in the mainline churches, or even to guess what role those churches themselves will play in the religious marketplace. It would be equally foolhardy to try to predict the future of those churches that have been created with the sole purpose of reaching out to a single generation. Even though the generations targeted by those churches may have in common a disappointment with the worship of mainline churches, their own children are starting from a different point. Children raised in the single-generation churches will not define themselves spiritually in terms of either distance or closeness to the historical mainline. They will define themselves, rather, in terms of their experience with the congregations of their parents. Children raised on "contemporary" worship of a type congenial to baby boomers may find themselves alienated from the worship that meant something to their boomer parents. Some will likely affirm that experience and want nothing more for themselves and their own offspring. But there is no American generation, so far as I know, that doesn't, to some extent, define itself in opposition to the parental generation.

Churches designed for seekers distant from or hostile to the historic churches speak to specific concerns not likely to be important to the seekers' own offspring. Worship newly minted to meet the needs of people in the late twentieth and early twenty-first centuries either will have to adapt in order to include the second generation or will have to sacrifice a good portion of that generation. And one mustn't exclude the possibility that mainline churches may prove attractive to some of those, whether because the historic churches represent independence from parents, or because the mainline will have managed to recover a biblical and theocentric worship.

Worship in the future is not likely to be uniform. There will continue to be variety, some of which will represent attempts to correct deficiencies elsewhere; some of which will represent failed experiments that nevertheless hang on; and some of which may represent the fact that there is a constituency for anything and everything, so that no way of worship ever dies out entirely. This variety shouldn't daunt us, as though it represents some kind of failure. We can't know what it represents in God's providence. But neither can we simply be content with whatever we're used to, as though we had no obligation to seek the most authentic worship possible for the churches for which we share responsibility.

For many years, in most mainline churches, what would happen on the following Sunday morning wasn't a big issue. Planning worship didn't require much time. As a pastor, I would provide the secretary with the Scriptures for the day, a sermon title, the names and numbers of three or four hymns, and maybe the text for a unison prayer or two. No big deal! The pastor could spend her or his larger energies for sermon preparation, or preparing to teach a class, or on pastoral or administrative work. Worship more or less took care of itself. Those times are, or ought to be, over.

Worship requires much more attention than most of us have been accustomed to give it. Simply imitating the worship of our childhood, or of our college years, or even the worship to which some are exposed in seminary is not enough. Those denominations that have been content for their pastors to learn worship by osmosis, or perhaps by a lecture or two thrown in at the end of the preaching course, need to rethink their priorities. The way we worship shapes the kind of church we shall become. It cannot be wise to leave what we shall become in the hands of those who have been trained to think that the way we worship is a matter of indifference.

The church can exist without denominational bureaucracies, without hierarchies, without buildings, without public approval, and even without degrees granted and official screenings of its future officers, but it cannot exist without worship. The church that ceases to worship ceases to be the church. The church that worships carelessly, without attention to what it's doing, may become something other than a Christian church. Or it may become one of those churches whose sectarian stridency is nourished by the poverty of its worship.

In the mainline churches of the future, ministers, musicians, educators, and church officers will do well to spend more rather than less time learning, pondering, consulting, reflecting, studying, designing, experimenting in the interests of an authentic, biblical worship that doesn't cut us off from the church catholic and the communion of saints, but prizes those relations; a worship that at the same time takes seriously the ways contemporary culture is reshaping people. They will spend more time, rather than less, on this first priority, on which everything else in the church's life ultimately depends. It will not be time wasted. What perhaps begins as duty will become delight.

Chapter 1

The So-Called "Worship Wars"

Several years ago, public television broadcast a series based on Joanna Trollope's novel *The Rector's Wife*. The setting is a small country parish of the Church of England. The rector has died—killed in an automobile accident, if I recall. A new rector has come, and he and his wife are doing their best to shake up this sleepy, complacent parish. In one scene, the new rector's wife is playing an electronic keyboard—some upbeat tune that's surely not in the Church of England hymnal—and singing at the top of her lungs. The artificial flowers on her hat quake as she hits the high notes. It may be that the new rector is shaking a tambourine. The stalwarts of the parish mumble their way through the unfamiliar ditty, looking acutely dismayed.

Another pastor, who'd seen this on television, told me that the sight of the rector and his wife practically doing handsprings had filled her with anxiety and uncertainty. She and her husband, copastors of a smallish Presbyterian congregation, had been trying to renew its worship life. At every step of the way, she had been haunted by doubt. Had she made herself as ridiculous as the vicar's wife? I confided that my own reaction had been almost exactly the same when I'd seen the drama.

Once upon a time, someone visiting a community could look up a church of her or his own denomination and drop in on Sunday morning in the expectation of finding something reasonably familiar. Lutherans were Lutherans, Methodists were Methodists, Presbyterians were Presbyterians. While certainly rural congregations were likely to worship differently than their urban cousins, nobody who took that into account would encounter many surprises. These days it's a little scary to visit an unknown congregation even of one's own denomination. At least, I find it scary, because there's no way of predicting what you may find. You may find Bach, the denominational hymnal, the *Kyrie*, the Peace, a Great Thanksgiving with sung Sanctus and Memorial Acclamation. You may find a hymnal published at mid-twentieth century or earlier, or a nondenominational hymnal that lurches between nostalgia and the charismatic movement and a service that hasn't changed since the '40s. Or you may find fifteen people gathered in a traditional sanctuary early in the morning, gamely trying to sing a praise song led by a closed-mouth guitarist who's never worshiped anywhere but the Assembly of God before he got this gig at Old First Church. Or it may be the fellowship hall filled with youngish people singing songs led by a professional ensemble of instrumentalists and vocalists, the songs projected on a screen, the minister in jeans and an open-necked shirt, playing the congregation for laughs. You can make up your own scenario. Mix and match from the above. The issue is, if you're new in town, you don't really know what you're getting into. One observer has noted that

> At one extreme, we find more or less listless performances of the official rites, conducted with a minimum of participation before scattered congregations in half-empty buildings—liturgies that reflect one pole of our culture: its impersonalism, privatization, consumerism, and functionalism. On the other extreme are celebrations that have acceded to the ideology of intimacy—celebrations marked by high levels of participation, low levels of formality, sitting loose to the requirements of authority and tradition, democratic in spirit, folksy in tone, open to everything but the past.[1]

These extremes and many gradations between them exist side by side in many mainline denominations. As long as we look the other way, these varieties of worship simply coexist. But it's hard to look the other way, particularly when we find ourselves dismayed by the way our neighbor's doing it. It's easy to say "live and let live," but the fact is that biblically and practically we know that the church is one body. Since people in other congregations have a way of moving around, and finding their way through our doors, their expectations have an impact on us. And since our folk don't stay put either, we have a stake in what's going on a long way from our neighborhood. Insofar as ways of worship shape the kinds of communities we shall become, denominations have a stake in the worship practices of all of their congregations. So, we find that "live and let live" is more than we can manage. We challenge each other, sometimes politely and carefully, sometimes in ways that stir up mutual antagonism. Everybody gets defensive, and then we have something like a "worship war."

THE FRUITS OF ANXIETY

Most wars, of whatever kind, stem from anxiety, and this one is no different. Everybody feels threatened. Those who are pioneering in new directions, whichever direction that may be, feel vulnerable. Those who find themselves paralyzed, hanging on with dear life to whatever is most familiar, feel that they've been challenged, put on the defensive. Whether we embrace change or recoil from it, not many feel really certain that they're in the right place. That, I think, is why we sound so certain. As someone advised the new preacher, "When in doubt, yell like hell!"

How has this situation come about? Why have worship practices shifted from an evolutionary pattern to a revolutionary pattern? How have things picked up so much speed, moved in such different directions? Much, I think, is rooted in anxiety. And the anxiety is a response to a culture that has changed around us, without giving us advance notice.

It's not that this cultural change is brand-new, a phenomenon of the 1990s or of the turn of the twenty-first century. It's been with us quite a while. But many who love the church, including its ordained officers, took a long time to notice it. When mainline denominational membership and attendance numbers began to drop in the early '60s, we were disappointed but didn't take it too seriously. Surely it was a fluke. Things would straighten out sooner or later. But now it's become later, and the decline hasn't reversed itself. About ten years ago, I think, many pastors in mainline denominations finally began to notice that something basic had changed in the church, and that it had to do with cultural change. The folks in the pews had begun to notice, too, that their numbers were fewer; Sunday morning was grayer, and new contributors were harder to find. Often, concerned lay members thought the problem was simply that they had the wrong pastor. If they could only get rid of this one, and get the pastor that all the ads in denominational journals seem to be looking for—that one "with a sense of humor"—well, then, things would pick up again. Talk about anxiety! Sometimes, the pastor wonders if the congregation doesn't have it figured right. As the pastor hears the praises of Reverend So-and-So, who used to pack the place back in 1958, he or she may experience severe self-doubt. Maybe the decline in numbers *is* the minister's fault. And so, the anxiety builds.

THE IMPACT OF CULTURAL CHANGE

Who can deny that ministers have been known to contribute to their own dis-ease? But apart from questions of individual competency, there's a larger framework that can't be left out of our diagnosis of the problem. The turmoil of the 1960s unearthed passions that have always been present in American culture. We are a people who established a nation by abolishing the king, the symbolic father. Even now, more than two centuries later, we can read Thomas Paine and his attacks on the tyranny of royal authority and our adrenaline begins to pump and our righteous indignation sets to quivering, and we're almost ready to take to the streets on behalf of the rights of "we, the people." So, when the civil rights movement and the antiwar movement turned the world upside down in the '60s, it was a replay of old patterns, deeply rooted in the national consciousness. And who played the role of the toppled monarch that time? Not the British royal family, and not just the governmental powers that ran the show inside the Washington beltway or in every rural county in Alabama. The "authority" that the rebellion mocked was, in fact, the whole of Western civilization. It was, after all, Western civilization that had produced an unequal, racist, bellicose, elitist society, the apparent source of all injustices. So this time, in the 1960s, Western civilization took the place of George III.

And where does Christianity fit in here? Those who rose in rebellion in the '60s, literally or figuratively, identified the historic churches of the West as creators, sponsors, cheerleaders, and chaplains of corrupt Western civilization. The old historic mainline denominations had served as a kind of informal, unofficial religious establishment. They were identified with corporate and government and military and cultural elites who had at least consented to the arrangement of an unjust society. If there was in fact religious wisdom to be found, it would not be in your local Presbyterian or Episcopal or Congregational church. Maybe an ashram in India. Maybe at your nearest Transcendental Meditation Center. But certainly not where your parents had taken you to Sunday school.

Some have identified the movements of the '60s as just another manifestation of the Great Awakenings that have occurred periodically in American history. A kind of religious intensity characterizes the '60s generation. There was even a Christian version of it, in the so-called "Jesus movement" of the era. But for the most part, this religious intensity moved outside the historic churches. In spite of the fact that most of the historic churches, at least on an official level, joined their voices in support of the civil rights movement and jumped on the antiwar bandwagon, they were identified with the enemy.

In 1960, it had been seven or eight years since my father brought home our family's first television set. In some ways, television has changed our culture even more profoundly than has the '60s generation. The invention of television parallels Gutenberg's invention of movable type. I don't want to add to the heaps of contempt that one can so easily pour upon the content of television. I'm not so much interested in the content as in the medium itself. Whatever the content, television changes the way people perceive things. While print media contribute to our seeing the world in a logical, orderly, linear sort of way, television reframes our experience. If you sit in a rather dark room where there's a television and don't look directly at the screen, you can detect a constant flickering. That's because the scene changes every few seconds. Not only are we processing information through images rather than words, we're speeding up the pace. I don't think that it's entirely accidental that it's a television culture which has become enamored of fast food. We've lost our patience.

About twenty-five years ago the editors of *Harper's* magazine decided to shorten the articles because they perceived that readers were no longer patient with full-length pieces. It's been a long time now since I dropped my subscription to *Harper's*, and I don't know what the policy is these days. But I do know that I myself have become impatient with articles in *The New York Times Magazine* that continue on to page 64 and then to page 78 and then to page 83, and then page 91, endlessly. My own attention span has shortened.

On the religion page of a newspaper there was a story about a church in Florida where you could drive in for worship without getting out of your car. That's not particularly new or unique, but this church guaranteed that it would all be over within twenty minutes. I don't know whether or not that was a money-back guarantee. Apparently, the theory was that people simply don't have the patience to spend any more time than that in worship.

THE NEW CULTURE

If people have shorter attention spans, and if they relate more to images than to words, and if a linear way of experiencing the world has given way to a more impressionistic way, then it's not hard to understand one of the reasons that mainline worship in the style of the '50s just doesn't work very well anymore. We could add to this picture a society that favors instant gratification. No wonder the television show *Who Wants to Be a Millionaire?* became such an instant hit! Why cultivate the art of waiting? Why cultivate the virtue of patience? A society geared to expect everything instantly will not be very welcoming to the idea that some things, including spiritual maturity, are not available in instant form. In the instant society, the profound meaning of the church's liturgy has to be available on first experiencing it. There's no patience for trying it on, growing into it, submitting to being reshaped by it over a lifetime.

Our culture is a paradoxical one. On the one hand, we're enormously "religious"—religious very much in the sense that Paul found the Athenians when he preached at the Areopagus (Acts 17). The shelves devoted to spirituality at Borders or Barnes & Noble are full of all kinds of things from the practice of witchcraft to Zen meditation to Jewish mysticism to goddess worship. We are enormously religious, yet most Americans live, for all practical purposes, as though they were atheists. Agnosticism is the default setting of contemporary society. From one postmodern perspective, at least, as best I understand it, there simply is no one story sufficient to hold within its grasp the whole of human experience. Next to the Bible you have to have the Bhagavad Gita or the Koran or the Greek tragedies or the writings of L. Ron Hubbard, or, preferably, all of them. One may be true for you, another may be true for me, but none has a claim on all of us. The word for that is relativism. The reasoning seems to be that since God has created all people as equals, every opinion is also equal. There's "your truth" and "my truth" and the two "truths" need never meet, which means that you and I never have to cross paths either. It's as though we inhabit separate universes.

This is a very broad, very sweeping, and surely far too general description of North American culture in the twenty-first century. To be even more sweeping, one word describes it all: modernization. At least, that's the word we use in North America. The rest of the world, particularly the developing world, might prefer to call it Americanization. From the United States we've exported movies, videotapes, CDs, Coca-Cola, blue jeans. Because of satellite transmissions, you can see MTV even in places where it's forbidden, such as Iran. Visiting overseas, it's sometimes hard to find a channel doing local broadcasting. You can watch *Cosby* reruns in Arabic or Hebrew or Japanese. CNN is everywhere. While to us this may seem like an affirmation of American creativity and the shrewdness of our sales strategies, to people in traditional cultures it feels like an invasion and an assault. Younger generations in most traditional cultures have been accustomed for aeons to showing respect for older generations, and particularly for those whose responsibility it is to pass on the cultural traditions from one generation to another. But the traditional cultures are less dazzling, less hypnotic than an image from MTV. They are less accessible than the special effects from a *Star Wars* movie. One reason that so many people in Muslim countries hate America (apart from the question of Israel) is that this instantly accessible American culture undermines local cultures. The people who had significant roles to play in a folk culture have been sidelined, if not discarded. Traditional roles and status systems have been upset. Religious faith has lost respect, along with those who have been responsible for passing it on.

Modernization actually has the same effect in North America, from which it has moved out to touch even reluctant and resistant societies around the world. In fact, the roots of modernization lie deep in the American experience. Americans have habitually been drawn to a kind of populism that scorns the authority of the learned and defiantly celebrates popular tastes. Indifference to history contributes to a sense of scorn for anyone or anything that's old, and anyone who dares to be critical of whatever is wildly fashionable at the moment. Disdain for formal learning, for history, and for the authority derived from them creates in us the expectation of mastering difficult and profound things effortlessly and in no time. It makes extravagant promises, just like the commercials. Whatever doesn't match the appetites of the new marketplace is cast aside. The dominance of entertainment and its link with commerce creates an expectation that everything has to be entertaining and either fun or profitable. How does the worship in your church stand up under those expectations?

Of course, this too-brief description of the culture of modernization is, in some ways, a caricature. Although from the point of view of the developing countries, North American culture may seem monochrome, entirely commercially driven, and entertainment oriented, those of us who live here know that it's not. There are cultures and subcultures, and the one I've described is only one subculture. And yet, because this subculture so dominates the public square, it seems to have triumphed, or at least to be on the verge of triumph. Does the church need to pay attention to this subculture, or not? If so, how do we pay attention to it?

ADAPTING TO A NEW CULTURE

Since the Second Vatican Council, the Roman Catholic Church has taken a great interest in what some have called inculturation or indigenization—in other words, adapting the church's liturgy to local cultures. Mission strategists have for longer than that asked similar questions. Should church buildings in Africa or India resemble country parish churches in England? Should new Christians in Indonesia or Japan learn to sing from the same hymnal popular in rural Missouri in the nineteenth century? To what extent can the church's worship borrow from the local culture without sacrificing clarity as to the claims and content of the Christian faith? The Lutheran World Federation has also taken an interest in issues related to inculturation. There seems to be a consensus that, in many cases, local symbols and customs can be refashioned for use within Christian worship. But there is always a caution. The local symbol or custom must not be so strongly associated with some other worldview that borrowing it runs the risk of distorting the Christian faith.

The differences of opinion among us centering on questions of worship also have to do with culture. Some argue that since our culture has changed, worship needs to change. Just as the church in North India or in Pakistan needs to find a way to be present to the local culture, the church in North America needs to find a way to be present to the new and emerging culture. On the other hand, there are some who reply that the risks of indigenization are too great. To adapt worship to a culture so shaped by entertainment and commercial models is likely to distort the gospel. Therefore, it's best to hang on to the familiar. Some others, I expect, would say that since it's not yet clear what the ultimate shape of the new and emerging culture will be, we should not become impatient or reckless, but should wait and see what develops.

In his classic work, *Christ and Culture,*[2] Richard Niebuhr described five models of how the church has understood the relationship between the gospel and the surrounding culture: Christ against culture, Christ of culture, Christ above culture, Christ and culture in paradox, and Christ the transformer of culture.

An example of Christ *against* culture might be the illegal, unregistered house churches in China. Their concern is first of all for the integrity, and the uncompromised purity, of the gospel. An example of the Christ *of* culture might be the church in Germany at the beginning of the Hitler era. It seemed as though loyalty to Christ and to German culture were one and the same, indistinguishable by most German Christians. Some might find examples of the Christ *of* culture in the United States, maybe in one of those Texas towns where the local folks don't see why there can't be a prayer "in Jesus' name" before the public high school football game.

Many Christians, I expect, are drawn to the image of Christ *transforming* culture. Mainline churches since the '60s have liked to think of themselves as working from within the culture to transform it toward peace and justice.

Those who set the gospel *against* culture run the risk that they will become entirely irrelevant to the culture. And the pattern of the Christ *of* culture creates an idol of culture, which is, as much as anything, a purely human fabrication. And yet, those who embrace culture in order to transform it run the risk that culture will transform them. None of Niebuhr's models is without difficulty. None offers a perfect or risk-free model. Wherever one finds oneself in the worship wars, there is a risk. There's risk of a walled-in, culture-rejecting sectarianism, inaccessible to the average person; risk of an uncritical embrace and idolatrous defense of the dominant cultural idiom; or risk of engaging in a noble, transforming mission that backfires.

THE WILLOW CREEK MODEL

One of the best known examples of a church that has attempted to relate the gospel to contemporary culture is the Willow Creek Community Church in South Barrington, Illinois. Some mainline church people (including ministers) who have investigated this model have celebrated it with unrestrained enthusiasm. A few have suggested that this model shows the way ahead for the mainline. Whatever one makes of Willow Creek, there's no question at all but that Bill Hybels, its founding pastor, has demonstrated a remarkably imaginative sense of mission. If he and others like him can teach us something, it's that living by grace may mean taking some big risks.

Willow Creek had its beginnings in an effort undertaken by Hybels and others to try to identify why young men between twenty-five and fifty didn't go to church. It's not that they were uninterested in recruiting people of other ages or genders, but they discerned that men between twenty-five and fifty were hardest to reach, and if they were successful in reaching that constituency, others would follow. So Hybels and colleagues went door to door asking certain questions. They wanted to know if the residents went to church, and if not, why not. They summarized the responses in five statements:[3]

1. Churches are always asking for money (yet nothing significant seems to be happening through the use of the money).
2. Church services are boring and lifeless.
3. Church services are predictable and repetitive.
4. Sermons are irrelevant to daily life as it is lived in the real world.
5. The pastor makes people feel guilty and ignorant, so they leave church feeling worse than when they entered the church doors.

After they'd gathered their data, the researchers set out to create a church specifically for this alienated constituency frequently missing from other churches.

Although Hybels didn't call it that, he was attempting to indige-
nize the gospel, to make it at home in that culture with which men
between twenty-five and fifty strongly identify. His strategy was to use
the popular culture to get a hearing with his targeted constituency. He
created a meeting place that resembled a mall, auditorium, or theater,
intentionally without the presence of Christian symbols. He borrowed
an entertainment model, using well-trained people and ensembles to
present music and drama to an audience. His model was certainly not
Christ *against* culture; at least, not against the culture of those he was
hoping to attract. Would he have said that it was Christ *transforming*
culture? Or did it happen that, despite all good intentions, it turned
out to be a matter of Christ becoming refashioned into an image
acceptable to a particular North American subculture?

CULTURES ARE NOT NEUTRAL

Here's where we find it rough going. Worship that is readily accessible to the culture can easily be captured by the culture. Worship that
resists the culture can easily find itself completely off the radar screen
of people who live in that culture. Is it possible for North American
popular culture to become a bearer of the gospel? Is culture, in and of
itself, neutral? A matter of indifference? Capable of carrying any and
all messages? Or does the nature of the culture itself inevitably have
an effect on its capacity for bearing sacred things? Does contemporary
North American popular culture carry within itself a worldview that
resists adaptation, and that, in fact, subtly subverts attempts to use it
as a vehicle for communicating the gospel?

Will any cultural medium do in the service of the gospel? Or is the
medium the message? Are cultural artifacts neutral, or do they subtly
shape, or misshape, the content they're intended to carry? For example, if music used with sacred texts sounds like the music used to sell
cars, will people hear the sacred text? Or will they hear, subliminally,
a message like that Mitsubishi commercial which carries the chanted
taunt, "I'm better than you are!" When a congregation sings "Amazing Grace!" to the tune of the theme song from *Gilligan's Island,* the
message hidden in the medium is that we are dealing with something
light and insubstantial. Music that is instantly accessible, and thus also
instantly forgettable, may subtly and unconsciously trivialize the text
it's meant to bear.

DRAWING A CROWD

I'm not sure that most who find themselves involved in "worship wars" frame the issues in quite that way. More likely, they frame the issues in terms of "what works." What works is likely to be what appeals to the tastes of the people you most want to attract to your church. It's certainly not a matter of indifference whether something "works" or not. We'd all like to believe that if we get it just right, our worship will attract people to it.

A friend used to tell me that it had been proven that if you permitted a child to choose exactly what she or he wanted to eat, without any censorship or coercion, they would sooner or later choose exactly the balanced diet you'd like for them. I hoped that he was right, and that this same healthy instinct was at work as people chose their spiritual diets. I hoped that some kind of intuitive sense would lead people to eschew spiritual junk food for what was truly spiritually nourishing. Unfortunately, I've since read that my friend's dietary theory is bunk. Given a choice between broccoli and potato chips, a child will likely choose potato chips again and again. There is no perfectly balanced inward disposition to choose what's healthy over what's pleasurable.

I presume that that's true for spiritual nourishment as well. You can draw people to worship in all sorts of ways, some of them profoundly unhealthy. The fact that a church draws a crowd tells us nothing. Drawing power is only one of several ways of evaluating whether or not worship "works." And yet, particularly when we're approaching desperation, it seems to be the only thing that really matters.

Among the other things that matter, of course, is the integrity of the gospel. In a commercialized culture, it seems that personal benefits measured in the short term are the measure of value. Can the gospel be fitted into that shoebox? Or, if the attempt is made, will the gospel inevitably be misshapen?

Even to raise the question of the integrity of the gospel is like waving a red flag. How dare anyone question whether anyone else's presentation of the gospel has integrity or not? And yet, even in the interest of democratic egalitarianism, this is not a question we can escape. The Lord Jesus who told his disciples that "the last will be first" and directed that "if anyone strikes you on the right cheek, turn the other also" and called his disciples to "deny themselves, and take up their cross and follow him" certainly didn't mean that his disciples were never to find enjoyment in ordinary living. But neither can he be understood to be saying that pursuing one's personal satisfactions before all else is the moral equivalent of denying oneself and taking up the cross. This is an extreme contrast, but not so very extreme in the terms of much of our postmodern culture, which is very often driven by the priority of the self. If nothing else, it illustrates the fact that issues of integrity are at stake. Integrity and drawing a crowd may mix, and they may not.

On the other hand, is simply sticking to the tried-and-true automatically equivalent to standing firm for the integrity of the gospel? Or does the integrity of the gospel sometimes require us to take risks, to push the envelope, to consider whether our firm grip on the gospel might be so possessive that it bends or crushes the very thing we're trying so hard to protect? Bored church members and empty pews are not an automatic guarantee that a particular congregation has preserved the gospel in its integrity. If "new occasions teach new duties," as James Russell Lowell's poem has it, then do we sacrifice integrity if we turn our backs on a changing cultural milieu?

It's not hard to find a bunker in which to take one's stand in order to fire a volley against our neighbor. Thus, "worship wars." The culture has changed, and it hasn't finished changing. Our privileged role as a kind of establishment church is over. Like the rest of white, middle-class, European civilization, our authority is under suspicion if not outright rejected. The same impulses of modernization that antagonize traditional cultures are transforming our own. We find ourselves caught between a desire to be relevant and the danger of being swallowed up by an all-devouring commercial culture, one oriented to entertainment of the kind accessible to the least discriminating.

Do we change? In what direction? How do we guard the integrity of the gospel without becoming withdrawn and sectarian? How do we guard it without imagining that the gospel belongs exclusively to us? How do we guard it without dismissing our obligation to those to whom God is calling through us? In so many congregations, it seems as though some imagine that their church is only for those already in it, or perhaps also for newcomers who are willing to help pay the bills while submitting quietly to the authority of those who dig in their heels against all change. How can we be the church for others while avoiding being a church that is a mile wide and an inch deep?

These are the big questions.

Chapter 2

What Folks Are Looking For

Most people leaving a service on Sunday morning are too polite to criticize. There are exceptions, of course, and every minister has had experience with them. Along with the handshake comes a complaint that the organ was too loud, or the new hymn impossible to sing, or there were noisy children in the sanctuary, or someone serving Communion was wearing too bright a dress, or the sound system wasn't adequate, or the lights were too bright or too dim. In most cases, these isolated complaints seize the pastor's attention but offer few clues about how to make worship better. It's possible to check the sound system and look into the lighting, but the organ that was too loud for one may be thrilling to another. The new hymn may have saved the day for some who have grown weary with the all-too-familiar.

The majority of those leaving the sanctuary on any given Sunday will smile and say something polite. They may be perfectly content.

If they attend worship regularly in that place, the likelihood is that they are at least reasonably satisfied. But the chances are that, in any congregation, a significant number will suffer from what Richard F. Ward has called "ritual boredom."[1] Some of those will not be in worship very often. Others may be found among the faithful who rarely miss a Sunday.

What is ritual boredom? It may be simply an inability to connect with what's happening in worship. The ambience of the service seems to send a message that none of this really matters. Or, if it should actually matter to these other people, it doesn't matter to me. For the ritually bored, it may seem that the service talks about God, but as one who is absent except in memory. It may seem as though the service is about history—the past—but not about anything happening now. Or it may appear that the whole point of this gathering is to motivate us to live more disciplined lives, or to get our thinking straight about moral questions or issues facing society. For the ritually bored, worship may seem like a conglomeration of things intended to serve as stimulating moral examples. It may seem as though the service is designed to cause us to summon from within ourselves the energies that will save us, and perhaps also others.

The ritually bored most often suffer in silence. Sometimes, however, they find their voices. It's then that ministers and worship committees may experience the pressure to create a "contemporary" service. If a minister and a worship committee should decide to honor such a request from church members, how would they go about it? What can they learn from the complaints of the ritually bored?

"WE DON'T GO TO CHURCH"

When the Willow Creek pioneers first went from door to door trying to discover people who didn't attend church, they heard about people's disappointments with worship. The respondents didn't say what they were looking *for*, but what they were reacting *against*. Bill Hybels and his colleagues collated the responses, noted a handful of statements that appeared frequently, and drew up a short list of common complaints. Next, they began to create a Sunday morning experience that deliberately set out to eliminate the causes for complaint. But it's one thing to avoid the turn-offs. Once they're eliminated, what's left?

Something needs to happen in that Sunday morning hour or so. What will it be? At that point, the Willow Creek pioneers were on their own. The door-to-door surveys could tell them what *not* to do, but couldn't tell them what they *ought* to do. Hybels and colleagues had to resort to their own experience and imaginations to design a Sunday assembly. Those surveyed knew what they didn't like, but few had enough experience to say what they might like.

Here is where we put a finger on the weakness of the marketing approach when it comes to matters of faith and worship. It presumes that people can tell you what they're looking for. Most people can't. The ritually bored members of a congregation may know only what they dislike. They may try to throw out a few suggestions, based on what they've heard about that new church on the edge of town where the huge crowds seem not to suffer from the same malady. Likewise, the unchurched seekers can list the things that repelled them when they last attended church, but they will have a harder time trying to stammer out what it is they're looking for. And even those who try to sketch out what they're looking for may describe something that falls far short of what the gospel offers.

Stanley Hauerwas makes a deliberately provocative statement. To those at a distance, and perhaps also to the ritually bored, he says, "Outside Christ and the church, you don't have the slightest idea what you're looking for. That's why you need us to reshape you and your desires."[2] At first appearance, this seems like an elitist statement. "You don't know what you're looking for. We do." But I don't think it's intended as elitist. The statement might very well be the voice of the apostles and martyrs, the prophets and saints, the great company of the faithful from all times and places—a voice addressed to all of us—to me, to you, to Stanley Hauerwas, to the people surveyed by the Willow Creek teams, to the ritually bored and the spiritually adrift and to various seekers who are clear only about what they don't like. "Outside Christ and the church, you don't have the slightest idea what you're looking for." In my case, that statement certainly proved true.

As an adolescent, raised with minimum exposure to the church and its faith, I knew very well what I didn't like about what I saw. In case I missed anything, others were quite willing to point out for me things about the church and its faith that were distasteful and compromising. There was the hypocrisy, which seemed clearly evident in the elder frequently called on to pray in public, but named in the newspaper for misappropriation of public funds. There was the sheer ordinariness of the people, and the fact that if they gave much thought to holy things, it wasn't evident. And there was the worship, which to some extent reflected the tastes peculiar to another generation than my own. I could see what I didn't like, but I was not in a position to say how things should be other than "not quite like this." It would take more than casual exposure to the church and its faith for me to begin to discern what I was looking for.

This seems not so vastly different from other aspects of life. If one should go from door to door interviewing high school seniors about what they are looking for in higher education, what kind of data would you expect to collect? What would the recent graduate say she or he wanted from an institution of higher education? Would she say that she wanted to be asked difficult questions and exposed to opinions that might shake her foundations, cause her to doubt everything she had always believed? Would he say that he wanted to be driven almost to tears by the difficulty of an assignment, which, in the end, would have the effect of vastly broadening his horizons? Would someone surveyed say that she wanted to stay up late sweating over a research paper that opened up a whole new vocational direction? Would any say that they wanted to discover not a way to earn a living, but a way to lead a cultured life? Not likely. It might be that the new high school graduate would say he or she wanted to learn how to make a good living, or acquire tools to meet and surpass the competition, or learn a useful profession, or use the opportunity to meet friends and make connections, or find romance or even a life partner.

And yet, those who have had a significant higher education experience might discover, in retrospect, that the most valuable thing they got from their college years was something they could not have predicted. What they got was something for which they had not been looking. In fact, apart from the experience of exposure to higher education, they could not even have known that what they would take away would be perhaps vastly different from anything they might have imagined to be desirable.

Is it reasonable to imagine that apart from a profound encounter with the gospel, anyone would be able to say what they might expect from such an encounter? People who go to church looking for one thing may, in time, discover something there of great value. But quite likely it will be different from anything they might have imagined they were looking for.

DREAMING UP A FAITH

The Christian faith is not something a spiritual seeker might dream up independently. It's not just a series of insights one might reach after a period of disciplined meditation or ardent research. Christian faith is rooted in the history of Israel and in the person of Jesus of Nazareth, crucified and risen. It cannot be abstracted from that history or that person so that it's reduced to a set of principles or ideas. In meditation or in study one might independently stumble on the Christian virtues, but one cannot stumble on the Christian faith. That faith cannot be separated from the itinerant teaching ministry in Galilee and Judea, from testimonies of Easter and Pentecost, from the crossing of the Red Sea and of Sinai. It's conceivable, though not statistically probable, that people who are spiritually hungry but know nothing of the Christian faith might say that they are looking for a way to lose their life in order to find it. But can you imagine someone saying that he or she is looking for a crucified and risen Savior?

Even those who know themselves to be looking for something are not likely to be able to say exactly what it is. Even if they can state their need with some precision, their sense of need cannot anticipate what's given in the gospel. The gospel is very likely to be an answer to questions that we hadn't known we needed to ask; a response to a need we had not been able to identify or define. As outrageous as it may seem on first encounter, Hauerwas has clearly articulated the claim of the church, that great cloud of witnesses: "Outside Christ and the church, you don't have the slightest idea what you're looking for. That's why you need us to reshape you and your desires." One observer remarks that

> Contemporary worship often approaches the Bible looking for advice and answers. The Bible can address such timely topics as "How to Deal with Sibling Rivalry: Jacob and Esau," "Jesus' Teachings on Adolescence," or "Solomon's Plan for Your IRA— Roth or Traditional?" The problem with this approach . . . is that God is not allowed to be more than or prior to our questions. And the truth is, many of our questions are so theologically malformed as to be uninteresting.[3]

TAKEN BY THE HAND

The Christian faith is not just a set of doctrines to be believed, or a set of scriptural texts to be learned. There are such things as Christian virtues, but they are not the faith itself, though they are derived from it. The Christian faith is a way of looking at things. Scripture invites us to imagine looking at our world and at ourselves through God's eyes. The church invites us to incorporate into our lives common practices that have helped people to be led ever deeper into faith—into confidence in God and in God's promises. The church (I'm speaking of an historic community here and not exclusively of the church as an institution) serves as mentor to those who will apprentice themselves to Jesus Christ. The church isn't where we arrive after we have settled everything in our minds and come to a perfect faith or a single-minded commitment. The church meets us at the point of our seeking. It offers to walk with us in our search. The church takes us by the hand and leads us to its Sovereign. In its role of mentor, it tells us Christ's story, reminds us of Christ's words, and invites us to live into that story and those words.

One of the practices that is key to the success of this apprenticeship is the practice of worship, and particularly of worship with the assembled congregation on Sunday, the Lord's Day, the day of resurrection. Worship is where we try on the gospel. Worship is where we become acquainted with the texture and weave of the gospel story. Worship is the place of meeting with the risen Lord. Worship not only expresses a faith already present, but it forms faith and nurtures it. That's why what happens in worship is important. We grow into the faith represented in our worship.

What sort of faith is represented in our worship? Leander Keck, former dean of Yale Divinity School, takes a stab at identifying it. He believes that the worship of most mainline churches is anthropocentric rather than theocentric.[4] What does that mean? It means that it's worship oriented to human beings rather than to God. In other words, you might say that it's worship designed to be useful.

Ministers and other church leaders often wonder whether they are about anything real. They are sensitive to charges that Christianity is otherworldly—"pie in the sky by-and-by." In the 1960s, the frequently heard accusation was that Christianity simply wasn't "relevant." Faced with the cultural crisis of that and the following decade, which severely tested the moral core of the nation as well as the integrity of the church, the charge of irrelevance cut to the quick. People struggling not only for their civil rights, but for an affirmation of their very dignity as human beings, had become martyrs. The war in Vietnam wracked the consciences of people who were both citizens and disciples of Jesus Christ.

Certainly the church must speak of these things, and where better to speak but in the context of worship? Worship frequently became a forum for the addressing of contemporary issues, both from the pulpit and in liturgical acts. As one cause after another clamored for equal attention, pastors felt pressed to prove that the Christian faith had something to say to people struggling with issues. And of course, it does. Nor was addressing issues from the pulpit a new thing. Whether new or well worn, the practice of lifting up matters of current concern is perfectly legitimate except when it forgets that all our preaching and worship are done as before God, not to prove that the faith is useful or relevant.

Human concerns cannot and should not be banished from worship, but they must not form the agenda for the weekly assembly for worship. Referring to Jesus' forty days of temptation in the wilderness before he began his ministry, Lesslie Newbigin says, "One could sum up the substance of the suggestions of the Evil One in the phrase . . . 'Begin by attending to the aspirations of the people.'" He adds,

> I am saying that authentic Christian thought and action begin not by attending to the aspirations of the people, not by answering the questions they are asking in their terms, not by offering solutions to the problems as the world sees them. It must begin and continue by attending to what God has done in the story of Israel and supremely in the story of Jesus Christ.[5]

RELEVANCE

I was flattered when a visitor to the worship of our church commented that it seemed as though our congregation had an ear open to the world. He had heard the content of preaching and prayers. It had not escaped his notice that we prayed not just for ourselves, but very specifically for all sorts of people and groups about whom one might read in that day's edition of the newspaper. The church needs to hear the cries of the world. In fact, the church's calling is to be, with the people of Israel, a "blessing to all the families of the earth" (Gen. 12:3). The church's work is to be a "royal priesthood," interceding with God on behalf of those who cannot or will not pray for themselves (1 Pet. 2:9). The Scripture drives us to be concerned with whole persons, and not just with the state of our own souls, or of theirs. As we read Scripture and hear it preached, the Lord of the Scripture frequently has a Word for us about the state of affairs in the world. Human concerns are no small matter, but, even as we bring all our humanity with us, we bring it before God. Our agenda is to be with God. God is the agenda for our worship. God is its beginning, its middle, and its ending.

If Leander Keck is right, many mainline churches have misperceived the nature of their responsibility to be attentive to the world. In their desire to be faithful to their calling to be a blessing "to all the families of the earth," they have tried to make their worship useful: useful in promoting awareness of issues, supporting good causes, stimulating "right" thinking, and stirring up energies for the pursuit of justice and social transformation. Or, on the other end of the ecclesiastical spectrum, worship may be useful in urging people to stand up for traditional morality, conventional gender roles, and familiar cultural mores. There are many ways of making worship relevant and useful. God is a part of it, of course, but most often in the role of cheerleader for an agenda set by and for one very human program or another. Whatever that agenda may be, it seems to be one more responsibility piled onto those who have come to worship. In addition to their ordinary daily responsibilities, they are called on to save the world and to save themselves. Though worshipers may recognize the nobility of the summons, they know that this agenda is beyond their power to accomplish.

Yes, of course, the Christian faith does have something to say about our life in the world and our obligations to one another. But it says these things always and first of all in a context of utter dependence on God's grace. The first agenda of worship is to lay aside any agendas of our own, including the need to prove that our faith is useful in the world. Worship finds its power when we set aside all other concerns, and lose ourselves, as Charles Wesley put it, "in wonder, love, and praise."[6]

I CANNOT SAVE MYSELF

Those who come to worship as seekers will be disappointed if, at the end, they are directed to find salvation within themselves. The ritually bored will continue to experience disappointment with worship that is anthropocentric, even when that worship turns the spotlight on them and their various needs. Worship that focuses on my needs is still anthropocentric. Worship that aims to be therapeutic or entertaining is anthropocentric by definition. I, the worshiper, stand at the center of those projects. However much I may be moved or engaged by the novelty of worship that focuses on me, it will in the end leave me spiritually malnourished. The cure for anthropocentric worship is not more anthropocentric worship, but worship that is theocentric— God-centered. It's not likely, though, that either the seeker or the ritually bored will know that, or be able to tell it to the pollster at the door. "Outside Christ and the church, you don't have the slightest idea what you're looking for."

The church that would serve as mentor to the seekers and the detached (the ritually bored) must know where it intends to lead them. Where it needs to lead them, and all of us, is to the crucified and risen Lord. The church's worship is not simply a subterfuge for evangelism. It isn't a recruitment device. But at its best, it embodies the gospel so *whole*-somely that one who participates in it will learn to see what the gospel is and what it is not. The embodiment of the gospel in our worship is the primary way we learn to live into the gospel, allowing it to form who we are becoming.

A member of Rabbi Abraham Heschel's congregation came to him with a complaint:

> Some of the members of the synagogue told him that the liturgy did not express what they felt. Would he please change it? Heschel wisely told them that it was not for the liturgy to express what they felt, it was for them to learn to feel what the liturgy expressed. As Jews they were to learn the drama and say it and "play it" over and over again until it captured their imagination and they assimilated it into the deepest places in their hearts. Then, and only then, would it be possible for them to live their own individual dramas.[7]

I believe that what the rabbi said is true for the Christian liturgy, too, when it's theocentric rather than anthropocentric. "Outside Christ and the church, you don't have the slightest idea what you're looking for." When any of us ask that the liturgy be reduced to the dimensions of our experience and our comprehension, we are asking for a smaller gospel, and a Christ who is less than the crucified, risen, and ascended Redeemer.

So why then is there so much dissatisfaction on the part of those who have, in fact, been present to the liturgy for year after year? Not to mention those whose exposure to it has been only occasional and even casual? I think the reason is that the liturgy to which we have often been exposed is a diminished liturgy in the first place. Whether labeled traditional or contemporary, the liturgy of mainline Protestants has often been, as Keck charged, anthropocentric rather than theocentric. It has been further compromised by having adapted, generations ago, to the need to be relevant to a culture shaped by Enlightenment principles. Our worship has drifted toward the didactic, turning even our prayers into moral lessons, or explanations of Scripture or of doctrine. We have been frightened of mystery, which we have identified as irrational, and therefore premodern, even superstitious. Doubting that the God of the Enlightenment is really free to act in the world, we have relegated God to a pious memory derived from times when faith was actually possible.

Deprived of confidence about the Great Things of our faith, we have become passionately certain about smaller things. We are certain about abortion rights or abortion wrongs; about what pronouns may be used or must be forbidden; about who can or cannot be ordained. (None of these issues is unimportant, but the ardor with which we embrace one view or another seems to substitute for a lost zeal for the Great Things.) Our worship has struggled to prove its usefulness. It has flattened out metaphor, explained the unexplainable, substituted moralistic formulas for deep encounters.

RESHAPING DESIRES

It may be that I exaggerate. Countless people have been nurtured by the worship of their congregations in spite of whatever weaknesses it may have. Certainly, I have found nourishment even in worship guilty of most of the above offenses. Nevertheless, I accuse myself of complicity in the kind of worship I have described. Not knowingly or willingly or obstinately, but swept along by the culture of mainstream Protestantism. This culture first began to be shaped generations ago, but only now has it reached a crisis point where its weaknesses have become inescapably evident.

Anthropocentric worship, shaped according to the idiom of the Enlightenment, cannot "reshape [us] and [our] desires," to return to the words of Stanley Hauerwas. And because it cannot, it leaves our desires intact, when those desires would profit most by being transformed. Anthropocentric worship makes a subtle offer to give us some of the things we're looking for, as though those things were the same as the gospel wants for us.

Just as it would be foolish to expect a recent high school graduate to define the objectives of higher education, it would be foolish to poll the ritually bored or seekers to define the purpose of corporate worship. If it were within their power to say what they were looking for, it would already be within their grasp. A person can really begin to put into words what she or he is looking for only when she or he has already encountered it. What worship ought to be can best be defined by consulting the experience of generations who have worshiped deeply.

Nevertheless, even those inexperienced in the faith may be able to articulate some of their longing, and that longing is worth our attention. Certainly not everyone yearns for the same thing, but I suspect a good many people in the opening years of the twenty-first century might tell us that, in our culture of superficial relationships, they long for some kind of community. People might say that they long for a sense of belonging to something or someone larger than themselves. They might speak of yearning for a connection with the sacred, or for inner peace, or for a sense of purpose, or for hope.

Christian folk will recognize these longings as familiar. They're not necessarily different from our own. We would say that we have experienced the fulfillment of some of these longings as we have grown into Christ. And yet, even as we have experienced their fulfillment in some measure, the fulfillment is nevertheless different from what we might have imagined. I longed for community, longed to belong to something greater than myself. I got the community of the local congregation, and with it the stresses and strains that belong to all forms of community. And I got, as well, a connection with and a belonging to the holy catholic church and the communion of saints, also imperfect communities, but immeasurably rich in spirit at the same time.

I wanted a connection with the sacred, and got it. But it was different than I might have imagined, too. The sacred seems very near at times. But I have also discovered that the sacred is not mine to define. God is self-defined and doesn't always fit my expectations of the sacred. I experience intimations of Christ's presence in praise and prayer; Scripture, sermon, and sacrament; service to others and in the service others have so generously offered to me. Nevertheless, God may require something of me rather than simply consoling me or delighting me. To belong to God can be, at times, a burden. And yet, paradoxically, there is a kind of joy even in the burden. I have learned as well that God is not at my command, and sometimes when I most seek God's presence, it's nowhere to be found. And yet, because I hold that presence in memory, I continue to anticipate it with confidence.

I sought inner peace, and when I take my spiritual temperature I can sense that peace in the foundational places, though it doesn't mean at all that I am always content with the way things are or the way I am.

I wanted a sense of purpose, and that I have found. I wanted to be able to hope to have confidence that the uttermost future will be one of light and song rather than blankness or horror. That hope, rooted in faith, has taken hold in me, even though I don't always have a firm grip on it.

My faith is sometimes strong, and sometimes weak. As I go to worship week by week, I sometimes bring my strength for others to lean on, and sometimes bring my weakness, needing others to hold me up. In worship, the longings so familiar to most if not all of humankind have been fulfilled in a sense, but also transformed. Not that Christians find those longings fully satisfied. Part of our experience has been to discover that for some things we must wait. But our waiting is not lonely or desperate, because we are waiting with each other, and there is One who waits with us.

ALMOST—BUT NOT QUITE

The more mature among us have also discovered that the fulfillment of these longings begins to be realized as we cultivate a long-term relationship. That relationship with God, through Christ, by the Holy Spirit, develops as we give ourselves to certain practices. Who, being introduced to these practices for the first time, would imagine the life-giving potential of keeping Sabbath? Of serving the neighbor? Of keeping the discipline of stewardship? Or keeping the discipline of prayer, or the discipline of learning to listen attentively to Scripture and preaching, or of looking for Christ in sacramental actions?

The curious paradox is that the faith of the church does offer people "what they're looking for," in a sense. But it's also more than and different from what folks are looking for, because "apart from Christ and the church you don't have the slightest idea what you're looking for." The question is whether the worship people find when they go to church embodies that faith adequately enough that people recognize that it connects to those longings in some way or other. Does our worship clarify what people are looking for, though they themselves didn't have all that clear an idea of what they were looking for? Does it invite a deeper apprenticeship to Jesus Christ? Does it have the power to reshape those longings in a pattern of discipleship?

A husband and wife were walking down the street in a city they were visiting while traveling. They had just come from a service of worship in a mainline congregation that had an excellent reputation. The building was lovely, the organ magnificent, the choral music fine. A man sitting next to them had introduced himself and extended a welcome. Nevertheless, the sermon had been preached without passion, the liturgy led in an almost perfunctory way. As they walked down the street, one said to the other, "Well, that wasn't too bad." No, not too bad, but it seemed sad that their experience visiting churches had caused "not too bad" to be a relatively high rating.

I love to go to church, and try very hard not to attend worship as a critic. Nevertheless, when I walk into a church as a stranger, it's true that very often I leave feeling as though I had come close to something of great value, but not close enough. If this were my experience alone, I would try to come to terms with the fact that I simply must have set my expectations too high. But this sort of experience is not mine alone. What is it that's missing?

THE PLAYFULNESS OF WORSHIP

When people enter deeply into worship, they lose track of time. When deeply engaged in it, worship seems a time-out-of-time. The anthropologist Victor Turner has written about worship as an occasion in which people leave behind the ordinary statuses and obligations of the everyday world. The things that ordinarily structure our lives recede into the background.[8] It's as though we enter into a new and different realm that is at odds with the structures that frame our usual existence. Worship as anti-structure, or as time-out-of-time, resembles nothing so much as it resembles play.

Have you watched children at play? Sometimes they like to dress up and act out some drama. They try on roles they have seen or fantasized about. They love chasing games, like hide-and-seek. Like children, adults can also forget about themselves when playing a game. Play pulls us out of ourselves, changes the way we perceive the passage of time, catches us up into a kind of delight that chases away worries and preoccupations. It's as though we are caught up into another world where time doesn't count, and we are immediately present to one another and the moment. Worship, at its best, is like that. There is, at bottom, a kind of playfulness in the worship of God.

Last Sunday at our church, one of the ministers invited the children forward for a few moments. She invited them to join her in a liturgical exercise that required them to stand up, move their hands and arms, and call out certain words to accompany the motions. It was delightful. In fact, I found myself wondering whether, after the children had gone back to their seats, the minister might invite the adults to stand up and engage in a similar exercise. But, of course, to no one's surprise, that didn't happen. So very often, we in mainline churches have lost the sense of worship as playfulness. Is it because we're afraid that playfulness is in opposition to seriousness? Or is it because we have so intellectualized our faith that we may as well leave our bodies at home?

Children, dressing up or pretending to dress up, try on roles. Worship can be a kind of trying on of roles. In reality, our individual faith waxes and wanes, vacillates between confidence and uncertainty. The liturgy invites us to try on the role of a faithful person. We can try on that role in several ways, by singing, speaking, moving, gesturing. We can try on the role of belonging to the great community of the faithful, gathered before the throne of God, with angels and archangels, and the whole company of heaven. We can try on the role of those who have been invited from east and west and from north and south to sit at the great Messianic banquet. We can try on the role of those who gather by the river that flows from the throne of God. The liturgy invites us to that playfulness that gives permission to imagine ourselves as God's royal priesthood, God's chosen people, a communion of saints for whom the boundary between time and eternity is permeable. It invites us to imagine ourselves as part of a healed creation, a new heaven and earth, in which nothing lies outside God's redemptive power, not even hell itself, where Christ has gone to preach to the prisoners (1 Pet. 3:19). That playfulness offers the opportunity to investigate the church's faith in the way that explorers investigate new territories. We can try the faith on for size. That exploration is at its playful best when we get up and move.

Worship so very often seems as though it's intended for the neck up. We go in, sit down in a pew facing toward the front, staring at the backs of the people in front of us. Other than standing to sing or, in a few blessed instances, to pass the Peace, we do not move. I long for movement! I don't want to applaud for the children's choir whose song praises God on my behalf, but sometimes, when the music resonates in my body as well as in my soul, I would like to sway just a little as we sing. In fact, I would like to sing more, and sometimes engage in prolonged singing, and include in our song some things old and some things new, some things borrowed and some things our very own. There are times when I would like to cast aside my northern European reserve and raise my hands. There are times, when the Holy Trinity is invoked, that I would relish making the sign of the cross, a reminder of my baptism. In fact, I allow myself to bend from the waist in reverence at the name of the Trinity, but I do so ever so slightly, so that no one shall notice who's not got an eye on my movements. I would like to go forward for Communion, and I would like to make this symbolic pilgrimage, this playful journey toward the kingdom of heaven, every Sunday, and I want to sing glad songs as I do it. I want to smell the aroma of bread and wine, and feel its texture and its taste on my tongue. I want to be bodily present in worship, and not just intellectually present.

I am not your wild-eyed, uninhibited person. I learned this longing to be bodily present in worship from my own role as presider at Holy Communion. It began to feel awkward, standing behind the holy table holding a book in my hand. So I found a stand to hold the text of the Great Prayer and set my hands free. I felt a freedom in the raising of my hands in the offering of this magnificent, Trinitarian prayer. As one who is now more often a worshiper in the congregation, I would like both to see this freedom, this bodily *presence*, in the presider, and to be invited to join in it myself.

When I can be present in worship that respects body and soul, heart and mind, then I believe I can discern the fullness, the *whole*-someness, the playfulness of the gospel, and in that journey to a time-out-of-time, I see there what I have been looking for, and more than what I have been looking for. In that service I discern a mentoring church, which is capable of taking by the hand those who hunger and thirst, and leading them to the crucified and risen Savior. Is there a name for that kind of worship? Would you call that worship traditional? Or would you call it contemporary?

Chapter 3

Is There Such a Thing as "Traditional Worship"?

Whenever I find myself in a hotel or motel room, one of the first things I do is to pick up the yellow pages. I leaf to the section labeled "Churches" and look to see what the ecclesiastical landscape looks like in those parts. Of course, my interest is first of all to see what the churches are saying about themselves in their ads, and particularly what they are saying about their worship.

Another interesting source of information in a strange city is the Saturday edition of the local newspaper; that's where the Religion section is. Many large metropolitan papers no longer seem to carry many church ads, but in smaller cities one can learn a great deal from these pages. I'm not sure many laypeople read the Religion page, but ministers do, even if only to check up on the competition.

In just the last few years, I've noticed something different in both the yellow pages ads and the Saturday Religion page ads: more and more churches have gone to multiple services. And very often, one of those services will be described as "contemporary" and the other as "traditional." Set side by side, what's labeled "traditional" doesn't come across very well. While "contemporary" sounds fresh, energetic, and tuned in, "traditional," by contrast, sounds, well, *not* contemporary. It's as though the churches are saying, "This is the up-to-date service, and that other is the out-of-date service."

What information does the label "traditional" actually give? The truth is that it doesn't really have any defined content. "Traditional" has only a comparative meaning, a fluctuating meaning, like the words "liberal" and "conservative." Neither of those words has any precise content, either. As we use them, they have little meaning except as to provide a contrast each with the other.

When the yellow pages uses the word "traditional" to describe worship, which tradition does it have in mind? Is it "tradition" as in African traditional religion? I don't think so. Is it the same tradition cherished by those Catholic parishes that advertise that they still use the pre-Vatican II Latin mass? I don't think so. Is it the tradition of those schismatic "Anglican" churches that cling to the 1928 Episcopal *Book of Common Prayer*? Not likely. At least in mainline Protestant churches, "traditional" usually means "the way we've always done it." Or, at least, "the way we've always done it except for when they did it differently before my time, or except for when it was done differently in the dark ages before people were as enlightened as they are now."

"Traditional" means nothing much more than "what we're used to." That little word in the yellow pages or the Saturday paper can mean everything from generic Protestant, circa 1950, to careful use of the most recent denominational service book. The "traditional" label really doesn't help. It doesn't tell us anything except to signal that there are at least two ways of worshiping in that place, and most of the older people are expected to be at guess-which-service.

"Traditional" isn't a word that has a positive resonance in the American psyche. There are exceptions, of course. Some respond positively to a phrase like "traditional values" or "traditional family values." But the deep and abiding American tradition is to be suspicious of tradition. Do you remember Tevye's song in the musical *Fiddler on the Roof*? Tevye sings about "Tradition!" We loved the music, but the play itself belittles tradition even as the music pretends to celebrate it.

APPEALING TO TRADITION

No one in America ever wins an argument by appealing to tradition, unless it's a very local, very parochial tradition. And if that's generally true, it's even more true for pastors. Whether in discussions about theology or worship, it does no good for a minister to appeal to John Calvin, Martin Luther, or John Wesley, nor to ancient doctrine, nor to church history, and very often it's even useless to appeal to Scripture. The minister who launches an appeal to these sources of tradition will likely be met by the response, "Yes, but *I feel.* . . ." Not what "I think" but what "I feel." And who would dare argue with feelings? The American conviction that all people are equal under God has evolved into the notion that all ideas are equal. Ideas reached with great labor, extensive dialogue, and intellectual effort, or that have withstood the tests of centuries are no less and no more authoritative than an idea picked up cheap yesterday and due to be dumped tomorrow.

In an early pastorate, an officer in the congregation explained to me that she believed in reincarnation. Foolishly, I suppose, I responded that one can't believe both in the doctrine of resurrection and the doctrine of reincarnation. "I can!" was the retort. And of course one can believe inconsistent things if the only arbiter is feeling.

When the question of worship comes up in a congregation, rarely will anyone win a hearing by appealing to the deep tradition[1] of the Great Church, or even the tradition of the Reformation. "Tradition" signifies what's not to be trusted. Voices from the past have no right to be heard in our discussion, no matter how frequently the same questions have surfaced over two millennia of Christian faith.

As one formed and shaped as an American myself, I can both understand and appreciate suspicion of tradition. The American Revolution was a revolt against a royal power that claimed an authority rooted in tradition. It was a tradition for there to be monarchies and dynasties and titled nobility, and it was a tradition for these few to run everything off the sweat of the many. It was a tradition for the Roman church to claim a divine authority that permitted no questioning, and sometimes the Protestant churches were equally presumptuous in claiming a similar authority for their own doctrine. There's more than enough reason for there to have developed in American culture a suspicion of tradition, and the people and causes served by the invocation of tradition.

Besides that, most of us have also been burned more than once by "traditionalism." In the minds of many people there is, perhaps, no distinction between tradition and traditionalism, but they're not the same thing. Traditionalism is doing the same thing over and over in spite of any objection for no particular reason except that it's a habit, and attempting to impose the same habits on others. "Tradition," on the other hand, comes from a Latin word, *traditio*, which refers to those things that have been handed on. In reference to worship, tradition simply refers to the church's accumulated experience in prayer, praise, thanksgiving, lament, Word, and sacrament. A church historian, writing about the people of his own denominational tradition, says that they

> belong to those groups in history who have tended to think of tradition as the dead hand of the past. We have regarded it not like the Orthodox as the Spirit at work in history but as the letter which kills response to the Spirit.[2]

No case can be made for traditionalism. It truly is the "dead hand of the past." But, to the extent that tradition is "the Spirit at work in history," it's deserving of attention and respect. Unless Christianity is purely local, and defined idiosyncratically and randomly, we are all accountable to the tradition. We are not bound by what has been handed on, but we cannot be indifferent to it. We have to respond to it one way or another. Worship today may introduce variations on the tradition, or critique the tradition, or reaffirm it, but it cannot escape accountability to the tradition. That's what it means to say, with the Creed, that the church is catholic, and that we believe in a communion of saints. We are not autonomous, but accountable to one another, and even those who have already died have a right to be heard among us, and even those who are yet to be born have to be taken into account. Any worship that makes a serious claim to be Christian is traditional in that sense.

That's one of the reasons the congregation I served most recently did not use the labels "contemporary" or "traditional" to describe different services, even though there were stylistic differences among the four services offered every weekend. No matter how much a service may be packaged in the garb of contemporary culture, if it's Christian it's rooted in the tradition. If it owes no debt to the tradition, then it can't really claim to be Christian.

WHICH TRADITION?

When a yellow pages ad describes a service as traditional, we're left guessing. Is it the tradition of the Reformation? The tradition of the American frontier? The tradition of the ecumenical consensus? The tradition of a broad, generic American Protestantism? There are multiple traditions, and it seems that there have always been multiple traditions. Some folks have liked to believe that if we could go back far enough (preferably as far as the New Testament), we would find only one pattern of worship, one tradition, and that from that one tradition have sprung all the many variations on it. But students of worship have become skeptical about that. The great likelihood is that variations in Christian worship have existed even from New Testament times. But those variations nevertheless do not obscure the fact that certain worship practices became evident in the New Testament. In particular, they are baptism, the reading and preaching of Scripture, and the Lord's Supper. In the New Testament, these practices are all linked to Jesus, and practiced in the various communities of the New Testament period. Whether these practices were uniform or not throughout the various communities, we have no way of knowing for sure.

In the second, third, and fourth centuries we begin to gather a little more evidence about how the worship life of the church developed. Again, there are many uncertainties. There was no uniformity. But once more, we see persisting the practice of baptism, the reading and preaching of Scripture, and the Eucharist. These things have been done as before God—which is to say, accompanied by prayer and praise—since New Testament times. There is a main stem of tradition that has been handed on. And that tradition has been received, critiqued, challenged, embroidered upon, and reformed over and over again both before and since the Reformation.

Gordon Lathrop, in his book *Holy Things* and again in his *Holy People*,[3] has developed a shorthand way of describing this deep tradition of worship. He speaks of Book, Bath, and Meal. Book, of course, refers to the reading of Scripture, and not only its reading but its interpretation, some kind of proclamation. Bath refers to baptism, whether preceded by teaching or followed by teaching. And Meal refers to the Lord's Supper, the Eucharist or Holy Communion. Lathrop would identify Book, Bath, and Meal as the essentials of Christian worship, or what he prefers to describe as the "central things." Alongside those he would add "attentiveness to the poor," because from early generations worshipers brought to worship alms to be distributed to the poor, and brought bread and wine from their own tables to be used in the Eucharist. What was not used was distributed to those who had need of it.

The "central things," then, are Book, Bath, Meal, attentiveness to the poor, and all done as before God—in other words, in a setting of prayer, praise, thanksgiving, and lamentation. These central things have persisted over the centuries everywhere the church has taken root, under many denominational banners and confessional traditions. They have been done in a variety of ways: sometimes elaborately, sometimes simply; sometimes carefully, sometimes carelessly; sometimes with appreciation for their capacity to carry the gospel, sometimes offhandedly or indifferently; sometimes with respect for their sign value, sometimes condescendingly. But nevertheless, this is the deep tradition. It's a tradition held in common by Protestants and Roman Catholics alike.

SHRINKING WHAT SHOULD BE LARGE

Unfortunately, over the centuries these central things have not always fared well. In various times and places, the churches have diminished, reduced, and made smaller Book, Bath, and Meal, one after another, each in turn. Baptism as union with Christ and the church was a terribly important threshold in New Testament times. By the second century we can see the continuing importance of baptism in that preparation for it had become more formally organized. A two-day fast both by the candidates and the members of the church in solidarity with them preceded baptism. Baptism itself led directly to the Eucharist. By the third century, baptismal preparation had developed more fully, and baptism of both infants and adults was linked with Easter rather than being repeated frequently throughout the year. The link with Easter was significant, because it highlighted the theme of dying and rising with Christ.

Certainly in the early centuries, baptism could be described as large in the ecology of the church's worship. The church prepared adult converts for baptism with great care, not only introducing them to doctrines and teachings, but, in careful stages, to the life of the community. If not outdoors in living water, baptism took place in pools, into which the convert descended as for burial and rose as one united to Christ in his death and resurrection. There was nothing perfunctory about it. The church welcomed the newly baptized with much rejoicing and an unforgettable introduction to their first Communion.

During the medieval period, baptismal fonts began to shrink. There were fewer adult converts, and so rarely if ever a need for a pool. The fonts remained large enough to immerse an infant. In the centuries since, the fonts have become smaller and smaller. In some Protestant churches it's hard even to locate the baptismal font, and in some cases there is none. Someone brings in a bowl strictly for the occasion. In some churches, the font is no larger than an ashtray. Remember ashtrays?

It's not only the size of the fonts, but the place baptism has in the life of the church that has been diminished. The link with Easter has largely disappeared. First, as Christianity became a nearly universal faith, there were no more adults to be baptized. Then, as the doctrine of original sin developed (understood as inherited guilt), people believed that an unbaptized child was in some kind of spiritual peril. Baptisms then began to be performed sooner and sooner after birth, which meant, of course, not in one or two great annual celebrations at Easter or Pentecost. Since they are seldom grouped, baptisms in our time are likely to occur on random Sundays, one at a time. More often than not, baptisms are done with little preparation and with a feeling of haste, the rite tucked in somewhere on Sunday morning early enough to send the children off to the nursery and frequently abbreviated so as not to take up too much time. Parents of children being baptized often receive no interpretation of the sacrament, no instruction in the meaning of the rite or the obligations undertaken. Congregations learn their baptismal theology from the movies. The Bath, in other words, has been made smaller and smaller.

The Book has also been made smaller. In the medieval church, preaching as an essential part of the Sunday service faded into near disuse. There were still preachers—and some *good* preachers, apparently—on the eve of the Reformation. But they were rare. In most ordinary parish churches there would be no sermon, or a poor excuse for one. Nor would the Scripture have been read in the vernacular. The only essential was the Eucharist. Chapter 5 will describe more fully the diminishment of the Eucharist in Protestant churches.

The Bath has been diminished among us; the Book became diminished before the Reformation; the Eucharist has also been made smaller, as we shall see. Today, the Book, the ministry of the Word, suffers from another kind of diminishment. It's diminished when preaching becomes separated from serious engagement with Scripture. It's diminished when the reading of Scripture and the preaching itself are widely separated in the service. It's diminished when there is only one reading from Scripture, so that the congregation doesn't hear one text set next to another, each providing a perspective on the other, as the lectionary texts are intended to do. It's diminished when the reading of Scripture itself becomes a casual and perfunctory thing, undertaken without preparation or due reverence. We witness this diminishment in apparently small but powerfully symbolic ways—when, for example, there is a huge Bible displayed on the Communion Table, never touched or read, but no such Bible in the pulpit. Or when there is a large Bible on the pulpit, but no one reads from it. Instead, Scripture is read from a small, hand-held Bible or a piece of paper. We witness the diminishment of the ministry of the Word when readers treat the Book casually and read it aloud carelessly. The services that we are likely to call "traditional" very typically do not address the diminishment of Book, Bath, and Meal, or attempt to remedy it.

PROGRAMMED BY FEAR OF IDOLATRY

There is perhaps another factor in the diminishment of Book, Bath, and Meal that's worth some reflection. Early Protestantism was obsessed with anxiety over idolatry. It was reacting, of course, against the popular religion of the medieval church. Everywhere in churches were not only stained-glass windows and stunningly colorful paintings, but also images. The people prayed before the images, lit candles there, and occasionally even dressed the images and carried them about in parades. There were similar displays of the consecrated Host. In nearly every church one could also find relics of saints, or at least objects that claimed to be the knucklebone of a saint, or a piece of the true cross. The first preaching of the Reformation was often a denunciation of these forms of popular religion, which seemed to break and scatter the devotion owed only to God.[4] The preachers denounced as idolatrous these acts of devotion offered to images and relics. In some places, this kind of preaching kindled very powerful feelings among the people, who took various measures to cleanse the churches of idolatry, sometimes in orderly and official ways, and occasionally by nothing short of mob action.

I don't disagree with those preachers or with their diagnosis. But fear never functions very well as a guideline. The fear of idolatry runs the risk of scorning the material world in favor of a so-called "spiritual" reality entirely separate from the material. Among Protestants, it's been common to quote John 4:23 as though Scripture proves that the best way of worship doesn't use physical things or engage the body at all. "But the hour is coming, and is now here, when the true worshipers will worship the Father in spirit and truth. . . ." But we have misunderstood it. This statement

> constitutes neither a polemic against external ritual and forms
> of worship, nor an argument in favor of the interiorization of
> worship, nor a criticism of the idea of "sacred space" per se. . . .
> True worship is rather a reorientation of one's worship through
> and in the presence of God in the messianic temple, Jesus.[5]

Where did we get the idea that "spirit" and the material world are in opposition to one another? That sort of dualism owes more to Greek thought, or Zoroastrianism, or the Manichaean heresy than it owes to biblical faith. It was, after all, the same John the evangelist who wrote, "And the Word became flesh and lived among us, and we have seen his glory" (John 1:14).

Christianity is based on the doctrine of the incarnation. Deep in Christian doctrine is the conviction that the Word has become flesh, that spirit can become manifested in material things—even such ordinary things as water, bread, and wine. Protestants have sometimes been programmed by so much anxiety about idolatry that we run the risk of creating a disincarnate spirituality that, at bottom, denies both the doctrine of creation and the doctrine of the incarnation and veers in the direction of Docetism, an early Christian heresy which held that Christ only *seemed* to be human. I suspect that this fear and loathing of idolatry, carried to an extreme, contributes to a suspicion of the sacraments. This is so even though sermons, hymns, and prayers also depend on the material—on the human voice, the human breath, the human body. They are not disembodied, pure spirit. Nor do we in any way have access to pure spirit apart from our embodied selves. What we call traditional may very well refer to a kind of worship that fears and loathes the body, an attitude that is neither biblical nor found in the deep tradition of the Great Church.

REDEFINING FAITH IN A CHANGED
AND CHANGING CULTURE

It seems sometimes as though American Protestants proceed under the presumption that the world can still best be described as divided between Catholic and Protestant, as though it remains urgent to define ourselves as over against Roman Catholics. They are Catholic, we are Protestant. Therefore, what they love, we hold in suspicion. If they're attached to a practice, such as weekly Eucharist, something must be wrong with it. But the fact is, we don't live any longer in a world where the urgent matter is for Protestants and Catholics to define themselves as over against each other. We live in a world that is aggressively agnostic on the one hand, and on the other pursues various forms of public and private religiosity that often verge on magic and superstition. Protestants and Catholics share this inhospitable environment. In contrast to our agnostic neighbors and our neighbors of various other sorts of religious commitments, Catholics and Protestants are kindred spirits. One of the things we share is the need to identify ourselves as Christians, to clarify for our own sakes and for the sake of others what kind of a people we are. We have available to us a wonderful resource, which I believe God has, in fact, provided us: Book, Bath, and Meal, and attentiveness to the poor. These form, in both the Catholic and Protestant ways of being, an underused resource.

In a recent essay in the journal *Perspectives*, Stephen Mathonnet-Vanderwell, a Reformed Church in America pastor in Pella, Iowa, reflected on the impact of postmodern culture on the Reformed tradition.[6] He was writing about the dramatic changes in our cultural environment, including the end of what we used to call "Christendom." He said,

> Under the assumptions of Christendom, Christians, especially Reformed Christians, spent so much time trying to locate the grace diffused in society that the concrete practices and commitments of the church were neglected. Here is an opportunity to recover the ecclesial structures and obligations of a covenant community.[7]

In other words, in a culture in which it was presumed that nearly everyone was Christian, the church used its considerable influence to exert pressure on society to reflect Christian values. That's where the church put its effort and its energy. The church didn't need to define itself vis-à-vis the larger society, or vis-à-vis vastly different religious traditions. But something has changed. Numerically, Christians may still be in a majority, but culturally we feel ourselves to be a minority. Secular and non-Christian religious cultures have made serious inroads even on the life of the church. The church no longer has the kind of influence that can hope to shape public policy simply by making official pronouncements. The church's voice is simply one among many others, and its voice is neither heard nor heeded in preference over the voices of others. Christians can no longer take either the church's mission or its identity for granted. If its mission, in some sense, defines who the church is, then it's also necessary to discern what that mission ought to be. That's a theological task, but not just an *academic* theological task, or even just an *intellectual* theological task. A theology of mission is worked out, in large part, in our primary theology, which is to say, in our worship. We will not be able to be faithful to our mission if we neglect those central things that shape our identity and distinguish us from the many religious and secular options. As Mathonnet-Vanderwell says, "Identity must be prior to mission. Without a strong sense of Christian identity, the church's mission quickly reverts to running errands for the world."[8]

In a post-Christendom age, we don't need to be fighting the Catholics, or, I would submit, fighting the fundamentalists as though either one posed the major threat to our being or our integrity as a church. What we need to be doing is recovering what Mathonnet-Vanderwell calls "the concrete practices and commitments of the church" that we've neglected. That means, first of all, unlocking our storehouse, opening the creaking doors, venturing inside to discover those things we have long ago stored away. In other words, we need to revisit the great tradition, the deep tradition, the central things—Book, Bath, Meal, and attentiveness to the poor.

THE CRUCIAL ROLE OF THE CHURCH

Why do we need to do that? I would suggest that we need to do that because in worship we encounter the primary theology of the faith. Just as the content of the faith shapes worship, worship shapes the content of faith. In other words, the tradition, those things we long to hand on to subsequent generations, is handed on first of all by participation in a community. Most of us, I concede, presume otherwise. I think it would be fair to say that the prevailing mythology is that every individual is on her own with the obligation to ferret out what's true, and then, if one feels the need of it, find a community that shares the same perspective. In other words, everyone is on an individual quest that may lead to a community, but only for those who want company. For some, of course, it does happen sort of like that. Some find the faith, then find the community. Or at least it may seem to work that way. I would argue that even the lone individual, reading his or her Bible in solitude, has in fact exposed himself or herself to the influence of the community, whose faith has been transmitted through Scripture.

From birth, human beings find themselves immersed in communities of meaning. Whether that meaning is oriented around faith, indifferent to faith, or hostile to faith, it influences the course of human development. However we may imagine that we are free and autonomous, we are not. It's popular these days to quote the African proverb, "It takes a whole village to raise a child." In fact, it is indeed communities that form children. New generations do not form themselves, nor are their parents the only influence shaping these young lives. The multiple communities of which we and our families are a part shape our perceptions of the world and our presumptions about the rules that govern it. We take these perceptions and presumptions so much for granted that we are not even aware of them. Lesslie Newbigin says,

> We need to attend to what has been taught us in recent years by the sociologists of knowledge about the social conditioning of belief. Every society depends for its coherence upon a set of what Peter Berger calls "plausibility structures," patterns of belief and practice accepted within a given society, which determine which beliefs are plausible to its members and which are not.[9]

The community of faith is the nurturing environment that kindles and forms faith. The community embodies the faith and, elegantly or clumsily, intentionally or haphazardly, passes it on both to subsequent generations and to seekers. In one of Isaac Bashevis Singer's novels, *The Penitent*, Joseph Shapiro, a returned Jew, makes that point. He says,

> Long after I had become a Jew with beard and earlocks, I still lacked faith. But faith gradually grew within me. The deeds must come first. Long before the child knows that it has a stomach, it wants to eat. Long before you reach total faith, you must act in a Jewish way. Jewishness leads to faith. I know now that there is a God.[10]

And,

> To become a believer is not so much to be instructed in what
> believers believe as to be inducted into what believers do, into
> the patterns of interaction and communication that give the
> community its specific identity, its characteristic ethos.[11]

Worship represents the tradition. It enacts the tradition rather than simply talking about it. For 150 years or so, American Christians have exposed children to Sunday schools. But Sunday schools and published curricula have not historically been the chief means of shaping the faith of new generations. The practices of the church, and particularly its ritual practices, have been the primary influence in passing the faith from one generation to another. Mark Searle suggests that

> Those socialized in their youth into the tradition but neglect-
> ing its ritual practice later in life will themselves continue to live
> off the tradition, identifying themselves in some sense as Chris-
> tians or Jews, but they are unlikely to be effective transmitters
> of that tradition to the next generation.[12]

The tradition—which is to say, the gospel that has been handed on—is embodied in practices, particularly ritual practices, and worship is the chief example. If worship is designed in such a way that it reduces ritual to mere rational content, or reduces it to forms that are not capable of bearing the weight of the tradition, we abdicate our responsibility. I don't know what every congregation means when they describe their service as "traditional worship," but if it means respecting the fact that the tradition must be embodied in viable ritual forms, I celebrate it. But if it means standing fast against all change, I fear for it. Or if it means complacently practicing what's been passed on without critical scrutiny in the light of the greater tradition, then I worry about it. There's something of great value in the tradition, but it's terribly easy to trash that tradition and hide it behind a shallow traditionalism.

Chapter 4

Is There Such a Thing as "Contemporary Worship"?

The early service, according to the newspaper ad, is "contemporary." What does that mean? Like the word "traditional" when used to describe worship, it has no meaning except when paired with the other. All worship that takes place in our time is contemporary. It may be a high Mass at St. Patrick's Cathedral, or an unprogrammed Friends' meeting, or an Eastern Orthodox liturgy, or three hymns, a sermon, a pastoral prayer, and an altar call at a small Baptist church outside Joplin, Missouri. If it's happening today, it's contemporary. All worship that is recognizably Christian is both contemporary and traditional.

Nevertheless, when we hear the word *contemporary* we know more or less how it's being used. It means something like the General Motors ad of a few years back: "It's not your father's Oldsmobile," that is, "It's not your parents' kind of church service." Why do you suppose it's so important to some to approach worship in an idiom that resembles, as little as possible, the idiom with which their parents are comfortable?

When I was about seventeen years old I began going to church. My parents belonged to that church, but they stayed home on Sunday mornings. A series of circumstances, mostly centered around contacts with friends, had turned me in the direction of the Christian faith. From exploring the faith more or less by myself, I moved toward the church to which my parents didn't go. I had been there some. Not to worship, but for vacation Bible school, and sometimes for Sunday school. It was a nice church, a well-kept building, large and attractive. But it had a distinctive odor about it. It smelled different than any other place I knew; different from home, different from school, different from the dime store or the drive-in. It smelled like old hymnals and old, unused Sunday school curriculum. Or maybe that wasn't it at all. But if I had had the words to describe it, I would have described it as the odor of the nineteenth century. The significant people in that place seemed to me to be rooted in a long-gone era. Their manners, their speech, their piety seemed to predate my parents' generation, which was, I've come to understand since, a rebellious one.

The art hanging in that church, what there was of it, was of the nineteenth-century romantic variety. And in that church we sang a lot of hymns from the nineteenth century. Not hard-core gospel songs, but things like "Stand Up, Stand Up for Jesus." Now that some time has passed, I can sing those hymns with some pleasure, as long as they're not offered as a steady diet. But back then, even though I couldn't have put it into words, I sensed that the church had somehow lost track of time. It was as though the significant leadership of that congregation would have liked to have dragged us all back to the previous century. My newfound faith was enough to keep me going, but I had to fight the impulse to cut and run. I knew that my future didn't lie in the nineteenth century.

I wonder if, for many of those born in the baby-boom generation or in the so-called "Generation X" that followed, there hasn't been a similar reaction. The church has had about it the aroma not of the nineteenth century, but of the twentieth century circa 1955. Whatever the year, it was a year that preceded the new era, the new consciousness that burst upon us beginning in the 1960s. Younger generations don't see 1955 as their future, just as I couldn't see the nineteenth century as mine. The year 1955 was before the television revolution took such hold as to reshape our consciousness. It was before Vietnam and Watergate; before our eyes were opened and we lost our innocence; before we learned that there's another side to the American success story; before we discovered that even the most benevolent institutions may, at times, betray us. It was before we learned that those who intend to do good may inadvertently do terrible harm.

A GENERATIONAL DIVIDE

What satisfied their parents well enough is not as likely to satisfy younger generations, at least not as consistently and not in the same numbers as forty years ago. I suspect also that for many people exposed to mainline churches in childhood, the parental generation appeared to sit rather lightly to their professed faith. Many so-called mainline Christians are in the habit of keeping our convictions and our passions about them pretty close to the chest. It may be the habit of northern European reserve. It may be the need to demonstrate middle-class respectability. We may feel deeply moved in worship. We may develop a strong sense of allegiance to the Christian faith. But we exhibit it, or speak of it, only with careful formality. We are suspicious of emotionalism, and that suspicion puts a leash on our expression of any feeling. We talk about our faith in terms of principles, values, even doctrines, but we don't tip our hand too much. The closer it lies to the heart, the more we're likely to conceal our faith. I wonder if in many cases our children have read us as really not caring very much. They know us as churchgoers, yes, and presume that it's a habit we learned in childhood. We conform to our own parents' expectations and the way they trained us, but our children can't see that our churchgoing has distinguished us from the general population, and they haven't been able to detect in us any passion about it. We espouse, for the most part, the values and the myths and the prejudices that are commonplace and conventional wherever we live.

Now, that's a harsh judgment, I know, and it's also a sweeping generalization. It's also true that most generations rebel in one way or another against the parental generation. But I suspect that there's some truth in the view that the religious and ethical commitments of the pre-1960 generations, for example, have not commended themselves very forcefully to our children. We have, perhaps, been too "cool." I don't mean too "with it," but too removed. There's been too little evidence that passion exists at the heart of our Christian faith.

Last Easter, one of the local television news shows in our city broadcast a few random interviews with people at a sunrise service at a local park. The interviewer asked some simple questions like, "What does Easter mean to you?" The people interviewed more often than not represented the generations that came to maturity in the 1950s. Their answers to that question were the kinds of answers that could have been given by a Jew, a Unitarian, a Buddhist, a follower of Wiccan religion, or in some cases even by an agnostic or an atheist. There was no evidence that the Easter story had any hold in the consciousness of the worshipers—or, perhaps more likely, no evidence that they were able or willing to speak about it.

This kind of low-profile faith, tending toward a generic religiosity, simply does not commend itself to people who are looking for a faith that claims them in heart and mind. For the generation that came of age before 1960, the default setting was to go to church. Individuals could figure out for themselves how seriously to take it and what meaning they were willing to derive from it. For younger generations, the default setting is to find some way of being "spiritual." They do not turn automatically to the church for help in their quest. And one reason they don't is because they see there conformity, but not passion. They see a kind of listless conventionality.

Those of us with deep attachments to the faith and the church know that's not all there is to it. We know where there's passion, we know where the gospel stands in sharp distinction to conventional culture. We know it, but apparently we haven't exhibited that knowledge in a compelling way to younger generations. It seems that our worship may serve to hide the very things we would most want younger generations to see and take hold of. It hides precious things, very often, behind our own discouragement and disappointment. Our worship may seem the ragged remnant of a departed spirit, a listless rehearsal of the day before yesterday.

PASSION!

A couple of years ago, author and professor of Christian education Rodger Nishioka published an article in the journal *Reformed Liturgy & Music*.[1] He had been meeting with focus groups of young adults, some of whom were in the church, some not. The agenda was to discuss worship. The author reported some of the same findings that others have reported. Young people are oriented to the visual, and most of our worship is not. Younger generations like big sounds, but not particularly the sounds of the organ. (While people born before 1940 may be attracted to organ concerts whether they are churchgoers or not, organ music seems alien to younger generations raised on electronically amplified music.)

Two things in particular stand out in the article. One is that the young people who described themselves as part of the church said that their biggest problem with the church was not with its worship, but with trying to connect. They wanted to be part of some small group within the congregation, but the opportunities were few or too broadly based to hold their interest. That squares pretty well with one of the attractive features of both the Willow Creek kind of churches and the New Paradigm churches like Vineyard, Hope Chapel, and Calvary Chapel. It's small-group life which, I suspect, really supports the loyalties and drives the growth of those who are drawn to those churches and find a place there. In the mainline, we have a really hard time in our age-diverse congregations creating the kind of small-group life that young adults are looking for. I know from experience that one can try and try, and success is elusive. Churches created exclusively for one generation have a certain advantage here. They can devote their entire program, budget, staff, and orientation to one particular constituency alone.

The second thing that stands out is that young adults said that what they were missing in worship was not so much a certain type of music or a certain way of proceeding, but rather passion. They sensed little or no passion in preaching or worship. What is passion? Passion isn't shouting or pounding the pulpit. Passion doesn't have to be noisy at all. Passion is deep personal engagement, which becomes apparent both in speech and in body language. Passion goes far beyond simply presenting religious data for the consideration of an audience. Passion is not a gimmick, but grows out of the spiritual lives of pastor and people. Passion is not the sole possession of any one style of preaching or worship. Where it is absent, no amount of skill or technique can compensate for it.

Those who claim that they miss passion in worship may not be making a fair assessment of the situation. The sense of something missing may relate to misperceptions by young adults of the faith exhibited (or not) by their own parents' generation. Or it may be that they have sensed, in many congregations, that ministers and members are plagued by their own disappointment and discouragement. It's almost a chicken-and-egg problem. If young adults were present in worship in larger numbers, perhaps their presence would encourage the exhibition of a passion that ordinarily seems to be hidden. And on the other hand, if passion for the faith came through loud and clear in a mainline congregation, perhaps young adults would gather around.

THE DIFFICULTY
OF DEFINING "CONTEMPORARY"

What do people (and particularly young adults) hear when they hear the word *contemporary* in relation to worship? I have done no scientific studies, but this is what I imagine they hear:

1. It's designed with them in mind rather than with their parents in mind.
2. It will be accessible—they won't be conspicuous if they don't know how to do something—and they won't have to figure out a dress code.
3. The music will be in an idiom they can understand (younger generations have deserted classical music in droves).
4. It won't have a hierarchical feeling to it.
5. No one will feel as though it's necessary to tiptoe or whisper.
6. It will move along at a fairly fast pace.
7. Some attempt will be made to engage the eyes as well as the ears.
8. It won't be necessary to know an esoteric language—it will be fairly basic.
9. For some, it will be something in which they can engage from a neutral distance. For others, it will show real confidence in the possibility of a changed life.

It's not too difficult to imagine how one might put together a service that satisfied some of those expectations, or at least came close. But what if you're in a congregation that has only one service and has no reasonable expectation of adding another? And if you should be in a position to add a service, would an additional service pull young people out of the existing service into one segregated by age? And is that pastorally wise or theologically acceptable? And (perhaps an even more difficult question), is it possible to create a service like that without "dumbing down" the gospel—to use Marva Dawn's phrase[2]—manipulating people, or trivializing the faith?

There's a second series of questions as well, based on the fact that not all members of the baby boom or Generation X or any other generation are alike, even though one can describe a generation's characteristics in general terms. There have been, for example, some movements of evangelical Protestants from these generations toward Eastern Orthodoxy. This certainly defies the apparent trend toward casual and informal worship making use of popular musical instruments and idioms. An article by a pastor in western Virginia, published in the newspaper for Virginia Baptists, described an appetite for liturgical worship that had surfaced among younger generations in his congregation.[3] If this happens among Southern Baptists, it's likely that the same impulse simply waits to be awakened elsewhere.

As for fast-paced worship, the hundreds and thousands of young people who flock to the Taizé community in France keep silent as long as fifteen minutes at a time, and do so with great dignity and discipline. There is also that surprising phenomenon of young adults who become attracted to classical music first heard as background music in movies, or who in great numbers bought CDs of Spanish monks singing Gregorian chant (quite possibly without knowing what it was).

Curiously enough, that primary example of success with younger adults, the Willow Creek seeker service, makes heavy use of the spoken word—testimonials, announcements, and sermons-in-disguise that make evangelistic pitches much longer than the average mainline sermon.

Add to that the perspective of an anthropologist like Victor Turner, who argues in effect that the very power of worship lies in its strangeness, in its set-apartness from the ordinary world.[4] A striking example of the drawing power of the unfamiliar is available to us by looking at the success of Protestant mission work in Korea or Latin America. More than a hundred years after the first missionaries took southern and midwestern worship patterns and gospel songs to those places, you can still see the contours of nineteenth-century American worship and music there. How does one explain such a phenomenon without taking into account that human beings may be attracted by the exotic?

When one takes into account these exceptions and anomalies, it's less obvious that there's one simple recipe for worship that appeals to younger generations or that worship which attracts must always be perfectly adapted to the cultures of the targeted generations.

HOW DIFFERENT IS WILLOW CREEK?

On a Sunday in late April, a colleague and I had the opportunity to attend the seeker service at Willow Creek. I had seen videotapes of that service, and the personal visit confirmed what I'd seen in the tapes. Everything was superbly done, and every move had been carefully thought out. Those people know what they're doing! And what they're doing is not about worship. It's about evangelism. Lester Ruth, in an article about Willow Creek, says that Bill Hybels and his colleagues who conceived that seeker service know very well that it's not worship.[5] Unfortunately, many mainline congregations that have used it as a model do not necessarily understand this. The Willow Creek seeker service is a contemporary version of the nineteenth-century tent meeting. In other words, when you don't expect the seeker to come to church, you create a space where he or she might come. Then you make your appeal as winsomely as possible.

When a seeker comes to the point of making a commitment, the intention is that she or he should move from the tent meeting to the sanctuary. In the case of Willow Creek, that movement would be from the weekend service to the weeknight service for believers. The seeker service was not conceived as a worship diet for the church any more than the tent meeting was. But just as the style of the tent meeting did in fact become the worship diet for some churches in the nineteenth century, the seeker service has, in our day, often replaced the Lord's Day service that both nurtures believers and enables the church to practice its "royal priesthood." Even at Willow Creek, according to G. A. Pritchard, it's likely that two-thirds of the committed attend only the Sunday seeker service.[6] Pritchard conducted interviews with a number of Willow Creek members. These are people who had made a Christian commitment and left behind their status as seekers. Pritchard reports that he "did not find any who had any relationships with other church members. "One [member] . . . had attended the church for more than nine years and had no involvement other than weekend services."[7] That movement from seeker service to service for the committed is a big movement and an important one, but often it does not happen.

Having heard so much about Willow Creek, I was surprised about some things:

1. I was surprised at the number of ushers who wore coats and ties, or heels and earrings.
2. I was surprised that the equivalent of the sermon was so long, so specifically evangelistic, and (as my colleague informed me) taken directly from a familiar model used by the Navigators.
3. I was surprised that the offering, from which visitors and seekers were excused, took such a conventional form. It involved the passing of the plate, so to speak, from row to row just like thousands of churches.
4. I was surprised in the use of a long prayer (which my colleague informed me followed a conventional evangelical model) designed to elicit a commitment. Although there was no altar call, those who had made a commitment were invited to raise their hands.
5. I was surprised that the "theme of the day," so well presented in drama and song (about the "hole in the heart," i.e., a sense that something was missing even when material success had been achieved), was dealt with in a rather superficial way.

The "message" was unmistakably Christian, but of that sort that sees the relationship between people and God in basically juridical terms, the terms of the courtroom. The glimpses of God I saw there were glimpses of a God who made the rules, but provides a way around them. Hell was a real threat, but this God seemed like a small God. In the sixteenth century, the great question of the day was how a sinner could make peace with a demanding and sometimes angry God. How big a role does such a question play in the lives of those between twenty-five and fifty at the dawn of the twenty-first century? Is there much anxiety about the prospect of having to pay some penalty in the afterlife? And if some evidence such anxiety, how typical are they?

My own intuitive impression is that if they were able to put their biggest spiritual and theological questions into words, secularized young and middle-aged adults would be much more likely to frame them in dynamic rather than juridical terms. In other words, the most troubling questions are more likely to be about the possibility of deep and lasting relationships, including a relationship with God (for those who would use that word), or whatever sacred reality might help to uncover one's deeper self.

In short, I was surprised that, apart from a dramatic difference in style, this gathering was remarkably like what I imagine a tent meeting to be like. Not too different, in substance, from some hard-edged evangelical services I've seen on public access television. The difference was the style. Theater seats. All kinds of dress, from ultra-casual to rather formal. State-of-the-art technology. Drama, well done. No Christian symbols, but then again, it didn't look too different from some evangelical megachurches I've seen. The music was played by a band in what I think was a kind of '70s, soft-rock style, while at an alternative service at the same hour designed for adults younger than Willow Creek's target audience, a band played a harder rock sound. The tone of the "service" tended to be impersonal, chaste. This is intentional, in order not to make the seeker feel crowded.

WHAT SHOULD WE DO AT FIRST CHURCH?

What's an ordinary middle-of-the-road mainline congregation supposed to do? At this point, the way we think through these issues becomes perilous. I would make a list of caveats:

1. Don't do anything out of desperation. Consumed with anxiety, folks seldom make good decisions.
2. Do understand what your strategy is. Are you engaged in a project that is basically about evangelism? Or is it to appeal to persons already present in your congregation?
3. If it's basically about evangelism, do you have both the plan and the resources to draw people from first introduction to something more substantial? Can you avoid confusing what is basically an evangelism strategy with the worship appropriate to a community of the faithful? In other words, do you have a plan that will draw new Christians into a deeper worship life than the contemporary equivalent of the tent meeting? Do you have the infrastructure to nurture people preparing to make commitments? Those having made a commitment? Small-group life, for example?

4. If it's about evangelism, do you know who your target audience is? What do you know about them? Who else in your community is reaching out to them, and how? Is everybody using the same method? Are those who are having great success churches that began as typical intergenerational congregations, or were they founded exclusively in the interests of serving a single generation?

5. If it's not about evangelism, but about pleasing some people within the present congregation, then the first thing to explore is why those people feel the need for an alternate way of worship.

I'm raising more questions here than I'm answering, I realize! My guess is that most mainline congregations that are considering adding a "contemporary" service have in mind primarily a constituency within their existing congregation, with the hope of attracting others like them. In some cases, the initiative comes from the pastor. In other cases, it comes from within the congregation. The temptation is to check out which church in the area has the most cars in the parking lot and do whatever they're doing. That's a mistake for several reasons, one being that it's probably not just the service that's filled the lot. (But if you're going to do that, don't forget to check out the parking lot at the local Catholic parish while you're at it.) If you can find the right people to ask, you might inquire about the loyalty of those who have been drawn to a rapidly growing congregation. Is there a high degree of loyalty once people become members, or is there a significant amount of drift from one to another among similar churches?

HOW TO DO IT

When considering strategies for your congregation, do you send out a questionnaire? I've become very dubious about written surveys. For one thing, they come back with strong opinions that cancel each other out. For another, they encourage people to expect that whatever they want, you will provide. So, the percentage who don't get what they want may feel betrayed. It's true as well that questionnaires often ask people for opinions that they're not well equipped to give. For example, if you ask "Do you prefer contemporary music or traditional music?" the answers will come back divided, and opinions will be strong. You will, after all, have offered two apparently contrasting and mutually exclusive choices. Second, once you ask about it, the stakes will be raised for those who are lobbying most fervently for change. If that change is not forthcoming, they are not likely to settle peacefully for the status quo. Third, the question is framed in such a way that people are invited to make a superficial response.

A better way is to meet with focus groups, that is, face to face with groups of people who can see and react to one another as well as to the questions you want to raise. Then, think through very carefully what questions will be put to the group. For example, you might frame a question about music like this: "What kind of music do you most appreciate to surround corporate confession?"[8] That question provides more context for a responsible answer. It makes clear from the beginning that music serves more than one purpose and that it is in fact a servant of worship rather than the be-all and end-all. This question is also open-ended enough that one doesn't have to choose between two starkly contrasting alternatives. Asked in a group setting, there's room for some give and take. People can hear what's precious to someone else, and they also learn the responsibility of communicating to others what they are thinking and feeling about these important matters. That's different than checking a box on a questionnaire. Also, it helps people to think through issues they may have thought about only superficially. Sometimes I'm not sure of my own opinion until I begin to articulate it, and then, offered in public, it's not always as compelling as I had imagined.

One church musician suggests that it's possible to go even further:

> It can be helpful to arrange sessions in which people representing different "taste groups" are invited to share perceptions, reactions, and provisional judgments. . . . One kind of exercise . . . is to arrange for church members with different musical tastes to meet in a group at regular intervals to share examples (probably in recorded form) of music they find worshipful.[9]

A leader can facilitate a discussion that explores what role this music might play in worship. How does it fit with particular themes in worship? Is it as appropriate for a body of people—a community—as for individuals? Members of the group ask questions of one another without making judgments.

> The group will naturally come to consider different norms and paradigms: worship as essentially casual and earthy in tone, or full of vitality; worship as something intensely quiet and "reverent" or else exuberant and ecstatic; worship as intensely personal or else public and formal; or as either ethical or mystical. . . . The whole structure of liturgy, and its variations, can come into view, along with criteria that the leader can help articulate, largely on the basis of what different liturgical practices themselves teach.[10]

Such a discussion can help members of the group consider what they think worship is all about in the first place. Is it adult education, softened by music? Is it therapy? Is it entertainment? Is it about recruitment of new members? Is God an absent party about whom we speak and sing? Or do we, in some way, actively expect God's presence? What helps us to experience that presence? What gets in the way? What's the difference between praise and confession? Thanksgiving and lament? The answers may surprise us. And, in any case, the conversation may help us move away from sharp dichotomies and politicized choices.

I suspect that the generations have more in common than they think they do. After all, some human issues never change. There's a hunger for God that persists throughout generations. That hunger is for a God who's more than my own face in the mirror. This hunger may manifest itself in different ways. It often surfaces particularly in the disjointed moments of our lives when circumstances lead to radical questioning of God. It may also surface in those glorious moments when the whole universe seems to dance in honor of its Creator. The hunger for God isn't just a hunger for ideas *about* God. It's a hunger for some kind of relationship *with* God. Whether they can articulate it or not, those who come to worship looking for a relationship *with* God will be disappointed if they're offered only ideas *about* God. Worship, of whatever "style," cannot bear the entire load of meeting this hunger. But it needs to be congruent with this hunger.

People of younger generations, and I suspect also many of the politely conforming older generations, come looking for God. They expect passion rather than cool detachment. They look for experience and relationship rather than ideas only. One can find those things among Pentecostals, for example, but they are also present, in a different way, in the deep tradition.

SORTING THINGS OUT

As a congregation considers its worship life, it's important to consider things like this: people can worship without hymnals or printed bulletins. It's even possible to sing and speak responsively and interactively without such things.

One can worship without the exclusive use of the organ to accompany singing. There is no consecrated instrument and there is no sacred rhythm that forbids a certain beat. When it comes to music, the only questions are: Is the music strong enough and free enough from stereotypes that it can carry the sacred texts? What are the subliminal messages of the music style? Does the music dominate the service, drive it, overpower it, or serve it? Is it a "vernacular" music?[11] In other words, is it appropriate to the abilities of the congregation? Is the music the people's song, rather than the song of a performance artist? Is it the people's song, in contrast to a music that is more complex and perhaps more sophisticated than untrained voices are accustomed to? Is the music appropriate to the movements of the service? Is it all upbeat? Or all restrained and quiet? Does the music reflect the experience and tastes of one generation only?

One can worship without the inflexibility of pews, and, I would argue, one probably ought to. One can worship without sitting in rows, our backs to each other. It is likely that reforms in worship will lead, eventually, to worship spaces that are architecturally appropriate. In the meantime, most of us have little choice but to live with the constraints imposed by architecture of another period and other sensibilities. Still, it's possible in most places to work around existing architecture, including fixed pews. Members can stand and face one another across a center aisle as they pray for their congregation and for the world, the face-to-face arrangement evoking a deeper sense of community and relatedness. Congregation members can, in many cases, get up from the pews and move forward to commune, or for laying on of hands or anointing, or for presenting their offerings or written prayer requests. A procession can include others than just the minister and the choir.

One can worship in all kinds of dress. People don't dress up these days to go out to eat. Whatever virtues there are in the "Sunday best," it's not essential for Christian worship.

What is essential, then? I believe Gordon Lathrop rightly identifies the essentials as Book, Bath, and Meal. These are the central things: the ministry of the Word, which is understood as Scripture read and preached; baptism, which follows teaching or precedes it; and the Lord's Supper. He adds to that "attentiveness to the poor," which can be seen in the giving of alms, prayer, commissioning to mission, and an awareness of the poor that is never far from attention in our preaching, praying, or planning.

I believe that one can evaluate any service, whether it calls itself "traditional" or "contemporary," by the same criteria. Does this service make large the central things, Book, Bath, Meal, attentiveness to the poor? Or does it contribute to the diminishment of one or more of those central things?

Another critical criterion is whether a service, whether called "traditional" or "contemporary," gives evidence that the congregation knows itself to be in the presence of a BIG God. Not necessarily a scary God. Not a threatening God. But a God big enough to keep the promises of redemption made in Christ. A God capable of bringing about the new creation promised in the resurrection. A God who's more than a mascot, more than a cheerleader, more than a therapist, more than an educator, more than the one who comes when I whistle to help me undo my messes.

Is the God worshiped in this service the God of whom we speak as Holy Trinity? The God who, by the power of the Spirit, draws us into God's own life through Christ, crucified and risen? The Trinity is not an add-on for those interested in theological niceties. Apart from God's self-revelation in Jesus Christ, our speculations about God and God's disposition toward us are futile. And apart from the action of the Holy Spirit, God's self-disclosure in Christ, crucified and risen, is simply religious information that we may take or leave. God moves toward us in Christ, and by the Spirit connects with us, lifting us into God's own life, which is, at its very heart and center, relational—Holy Trinity. Worship that is profoundly Christian will be shaped in form and content by a Trinitarian faith.

In evaluating any service of worship, however we may describe it, we must ask whether it provides ample opportunity to offer praise and thanks directly to God, and also whether there is room for naming and lamenting our loss and sadness, the hurt and brokenness of the world. Does the service offer hope? Not the illusion that everything is getting better, or that the situation justifies an unmixed optimism, but a powerful hope in God and God's purposes set against a realistic assessment of a world that is both magnificent and terrible, beautiful and ugly, delightful and threatening.

I think there's no question that worship as we generally experience it in mainline churches needs reform. What's not so certain is what reform would look like. Is it merely a matter of rearranging the furniture and getting out the tambourines? Or does it require beginning at the center rather than at the edges? Does it have to do, first of all, with the way we make use of the central things? I think we have the resources for a reform of our worship that is more than superficial. It requires a delicate attentiveness, at one and the same time, to the culture around us and to the deep tradition of the church. It requires boldness and caution—an uncomfortable combination at best.

A friend once told me that her impression was that people who needed to hear a word of grace often heard only a word of judgment, and people who needed to hear a word of judgment heard only a word of grace. Might it not also be true that those who most need to be bold often gravitate toward caution, and those who most need to be cautious throw all caution to the winds? The times call for caution and boldness, boldness and caution, at one and the same time.

Chapter 5

The Ecology of Word and Sacrament

A little volume published in the 1960s advances ideas that still need to be heard by most of the church today. It's called *Pulpit and Table*,[1] by Howard Hageman, a pastor in the Reformed Church of America who was at the time of publication the president of New Brunswick Seminary. Though published nearly forty years ago, it's still a relevant piece of writing. Hageman raised a question in that book with which Protestants still need to deal. He said, "A church that loses the Word must finally lose the Sacrament. But is it not equally true that a church which loses the Sacrament must finally lose the Word?"

What was he getting at? Clearly, at the time of the Protestant Reformation, one issue of great importance to the reformers as they attempted to renew worship was that the sacrament not be celebrated unless accompanied by the Word. John Calvin and others of the reformers were reacting to what they had seen as the deterioration of worship in the medieval church. Preaching took place in the medieval church, of course, and sometimes fine preaching, mostly by itinerant preachers. But at Mass in the ordinary parish church, Scripture would be read in Latin, and there would be no sermon. Many parish priests didn't know much Scripture, and so even if they did preach, their sermons would not be biblically based. Others weren't educated at all and simply learned the text of the Mass by rote. The ministry of the Word had been reduced to a faint voice.

As the Word became diminished, the Eucharist also became distorted. Without the Word, the Eucharist lost its moorings in the gospel story. It lost its resemblance to a meal and became reduced to a single dimension—that of a sacrifice. The priest prayed the eucharistic prayer at a distance from the congregation, in a low voice, from behind a screen. It was enough for the congregation simply to be present. There was no role for the people, who stood mute or said their rosaries waiting for the ringing of the sanctuary bell and the elevation of the transubstantiated Host. Seeing the Host held high for their observation became the people's Communion. The clergy considered this enough, and they did not even encourage the people to come to the altar rail to eat or drink.

Finally, when it became rare for anyone to take Communion at all, the Lateran Council of 1215 found it necessary to require that people commune once a year at Easter, and that they go to confession beforehand to cleanse their souls. The diminishment of the Word had permitted the Eucharist to slip from a meal eaten in common to an almost magical ritual expected to earn some kind of merit in heaven. In fact, it was often celebrated in private, by the priest alone, in exchange for offerings. When people did commune, they received the bread alone, without the cup, in the company of a pious few. The loss of the Word—the loss of familiarity with Scripture and its regular proclamation—resulted in the disfiguring of the Eucharist. It became mired in privatization and superstition.

THE PROTESTANT REFORMERS' PROJECT

The Reformation occurred in a period of transition, in some ways not entirely unlike our own. As in every such time, the Reformers wanted to renew the worship life of the church. Many folks have vast misconceptions about their project of renewing worship. They imagine that the Protestant reformers wanted to replace the Mass with preaching alone. This was certainly not true of either Luther or Calvin. In the case of John Calvin, whose work has shaped Presbyterian, Reformed, and Congregational churches and others that have been influenced by them, his project was to restore both Word and sacrament to their proper dignity. Calvin envisioned a weekly service that would include both the faithful reading and preaching of the Word and a celebration of the Holy Meal by the entire assembled community. It was the city council of Geneva that vetoed Calvin's plan. It may have been that a shift from communing on an average of once or maybe twice a year to fifty-two times was more than the city fathers could imagine—perhaps especially because they still retained some of the medieval anxiety about accidentally committing some sacrilege with the consecrated bread, and now the cup besides, since the Reformers had restored it to the people as well. So, Calvin had to settle for quarterly Communion in Geneva—Christmas, Easter, Pentecost, and early fall.

Martin Luther also had in mind a service that would include both preaching and Eucharist as the norm for Sunday worship. He experienced more initial success than Calvin in realizing this ideal, but it was not to last.

> By the end of the eighteenth century, the weekly eucharist had disappeared in Leipzig, largely a victim of the Enlightenment. It was still common to have a weekly eucharist in Lutheran Sweden but this slowly eroded during the nineteenth century.[2]

John Wesley had urged his followers toward a service that united preaching and Holy Communion. Wesley, a popular preacher, sought opportunities to commune on Sundays wherever he traveled. It was not due to some theological principle that his ideal has not been realized, but circumstance. The early Methodist Societies in England were not intended to be churches—since Wesley's hope was that his followers would remain in communion with the Church of England—so they gathered around the Word, but didn't ordain their own ministers or celebrate the Lord's Supper. Translated into an American setting, the Wesleyan movement faced a shortage of ministers, which resulted in itinerant preachers visiting scattered gatherings of believers, often at long intervals. In the absence of ministers, these small congregations developed a piety in which sacraments played only an occasional part.

Infrequent Communion became the pattern in most of Protestantism, not because of any theological principle but because of circumstances. In the first generations, those circumstances rose out of the situation of people making the transition from the pre-Reformation church to the post-Reformation church. But the pattern of infrequent Communion has become the standard pattern among the majority of Protestants, and those who imagine that infrequency is rooted in principle strain the imagination trying to identify what the principle might be.

SHRINKING THE EUCHARIST

A notable twentieth-century Swiss theologian has reflected that Liberal Protestantism

> has never known quite what to do about the sacraments and . . .
> is challenged more strongly by the sacraments than by anything
> else.[3]

Just as baptism has become smaller and smaller, the Eucharist has also become smaller among us. First it became occasional rather than weekly, as the majority of the Reformers desired it and as it had been in the first centuries of Christian history. Then over the years we have frequently made it into an occasion for preaching a second sermon or for offering a lecture on sacramental theology. Instead of praying the Eucharist, we have taught the Eucharist. The preacher may go from pulpit to table, explaining things along the way. The Puritans, in particular, contributed to a suspicion of actions in worship in preference for words. The resulting didacticism has plagued us, and still plagues us, and it contributes to making the Eucharist smaller.

Another factor in making smaller what ought to be larger is that the eucharistic prayer, the Great Prayer of Thanksgiving, has often been reduced to a purely private prayer of the presider's own composition. An extemporaneous prayer of thanksgiving is not a problem in and of itself, except when the presider is ignorant of or indifferent to the way the church has historically framed its prayer at the holy table. The Trinitarian form and content is often lost. Neither a general prayer with allusions to the institution of the Supper or a simple table grace is sufficient to convey the fullness of the gift God offers in the sacrament. Simply repeating the Words of Institution with no thanksgiving at all certainly omits a vital part of what Jesus referred to when he said, "Do this. . . ." We may celebrate the Supper elaborately or with great simplicity, but when we reduce it to mere obedience to a command, or to a perfunctory distribution of bread and wine, we minimize it. When we shrink, shrivel, and diminish our eucharistic practice, its smallness and its obscurity reduce its value as a large and powerful sign of God's grace and promise.

In the church in Geneva, the mother church of all those who belong to the Reformed family, communicants went forward to the holy table where they stood or sometimes knelt. In Scotland and in The Netherlands, communicants in Reformed churches went forward to sit at actual tables that had been prepared for them. The Zurich reformer Zwingli, who taught a low sacramental theology, had introduced the serving of Communion in the pews. The English Independents (later Congregationalists) also preferred pew Communion, which was stoutly resisted in Scotland until the first quarter of the nineteenth century. This became the standard practice in most English-speaking churches other than the Episcopal church, the Methodist church that derived from it, and the Lutherans, who brought their practice of altar Communion with them from Europe. Pew Communion has some virtues, in conception at least. One can imagine neighbor serving neighbor, each a priest to the other. But in practice, it doesn't often work that way. No matter how carefully one gives instructions, each communicant insists on balancing the tray in his or her own hands, and serving himself or herself. The practice of serving ourselves passively seated in the pews contributes to making the Eucharist smaller.

The absence of a real loaf also contributes to the diminishment of the Supper. For centuries, the ancient churches both East and West used an ordinary local bread, which was leavened. Unleavened wafers or tiny crackers are not bread. And Mr. Welch's invention, a chemical process to halt the process of fermentation, has contributed to the diminishment of the Eucharist when grape juice has entirely displaced wine and even made the use of the biblical drink a matter of controversy.

The Eucharist becomes smaller when we break its connection with the poor. In the early church, people brought to worship bread and wine as their offering. When the service was over, the officers of the church took whatever hadn't been needed for the Lord's Supper (and therefore had not been taken to the holy table to be blessed, broken, and given) to be delivered to those who had need of it for food and drink. Members of the assembly also brought alms to be distributed among the poor. The weekly gathering for Word and sacrament had a clear and unmistakable link with those who were in need and at risk. The church's worship led it into the world, bearing the most basic of gifts, essential for the survival of the vulnerable. This historic link has very often become faint in contemporary churches. When we neglect spoken prayers for the suffering, when we neglect to use public worship as an occasion to commission people to ministries that serve the vulnerable, when our preaching seems not to notice the poor or the voiceless, and when our stewardship of resources makes small the priority of ministry to those outside the congregation, we weaken the connection between the Lord's hospitality at the table in the church and the Lord's hospitality to the poor, extended to them through us.

One other factor has contributed to making the Eucharist smaller among us. In late medieval piety, the Eucharist was a somber affair, oriented to Jesus' death, to the cross, and to human sin that had nailed him there. The tone of the Lord's Supper was penitential. That same penitential piety found its way into Protestantism unchallenged and reigned supreme until it began to turn around at mid-twentieth century. The Lord's Supper as a replay of the Last Supper has contributed to and been a part of the diminishment of the Holy Meal among us. We have forgotten or neglected the early church's experience of meeting the risen Lord at Table.

Infrequency of celebration, of course, means that we forget how to do it. When Communion is quarterly, or even monthly, it is awkward every time for ministers, for those serving, and everyone else alike. Where do I stand? What do I say? When do I do what? Awkwardness throws us off balance and contributes to our uneasiness with more frequent Communion.

THE RISK OF DISTORTING
THE SERVICE OF THE WORD

Back to Howard Hageman's pointed question: "A church that loses the Word must finally lose the Sacrament. But is it not equally true that a church which loses the Sacrament must finally lose the Word?" I think he's right. When the sacrament is diminished, and the Word alone remains at the center of our worship, the Word runs the risk of distortion. When the table is absent—with its representation of

Christ's death and resurrection, with its representation of grace, with its offer of life as a gift—or when it is marginalized, preaching can easily degenerate into some other sort of public speech than a true ministry of the Word. Gordon Lathrop says that preaching needs to say the same thing that baptism and the Eucharist say.[4] Because, you see, preaching itself is, or ought to be, sacramental. Through human speech and personality, Christ the Word becomes present to the people of God. But this sacramental action is short-circuited when preaching becomes another kind of public speech—propaganda, or therapy, or setting out a political program, or promoting a good cause or a denominational project, or adult education, or even Bible study. When preaching becomes lecture or book review or scolding or desperate to be "useful" in any way, it falls short of what it's meant to be.

There is an ecology of Word and sacrament that is not to be scorned. Word and sacrament together engage the whole person: the intellect, the emotions, the heart, the spirit, the mind, the will, the entire self. Chiseled apart, the Word threatens to become a head trip and the Eucharist to slide into superstition or sentimentality or reluctant obligation.

On the Sunday after Christmas, while visiting friends, I worshiped in a church near their home. The text for the day was the story of the twelve-year-old Jesus left behind in the temple at Jerusalem while his parents worried themselves sick looking for him. The preacher treated it as a morality tale in which the story was turned upside down in order to portray Jesus as a model child, obedient to his parents. That may seem a ridiculous trivialization of Scripture. But it's not altogether unusual to find similar uses of biblical texts even by those who aspire to be biblical preachers. In a community in which I used to live, some interdenominational committee occasionally sent me a whole packet of texts to be used to preach sermons on "Traffic Safety Sabbath."

Some years ago, I heard James Sanders say about preaching, "Theologize, don't moralize!" In other words, look for God in the text rather than some simplistic moral lesson. It's moralizing when the preacher expects the energy for redemption to come from the congregation rather than from God. The energy coming from God's side may very well stimulate an energetic response, but our own redemption and the redemption of the world moves from God toward us. The good news is that we don't have to do what we cannot do—save the world all by ourselves. Preaching that is not set next to the sacraments, and that isn't attentive to the Word in the sacraments, is particularly at risk of descending into moralizing. Sometimes we who preach become almost desperate to prove that our preaching is "relevant," to use that ubiquitous word from the '60s. And in our desperation we're tempted to turn every text into a lesson to be learned. In the process, we may lose the Word who is more than words, more than lessons, but rather One who becomes present to us to reshape us in ways not so easily categorized.

"WON'T JESUS MISS US?"

I know a couple who have a grown son who is developmentally disabled. The family is active in the church, and they seldom miss worship. One winter Sunday morning they awakened late and breakfast took longer than usual, and everything seemed a little off-balance. The parents decided, for this one Sunday, to stay home from church. They told their son, who seemed to accept their decision. But after pondering this news for a while, he asked his father, "Won't Jesus miss us?"

I think that this young man may have grasped something that many who are more intellectually sophisticated have not quite grasped. The Sunday assembly is about meeting the risen Lord. Such a meeting is not possible in the natural order of things, but the action of the Holy Spirit brings about what is not conceivable in ordinary ways of thinking. This meeting is effected by the vehicles God has given us: by Word and by sacrament. In the case of the developmentally disabled, the words of liturgy and sermon may not strike home very precisely. But Jesus' presence in sacramental actions may be discerned nevertheless. "Won't Jesus miss us?"

When I visit churches these days, it's very common to find that some kind of worship bag or worship kit has been prepared for children. Christian educators believe that children should be present in worship. Worship is a skill to be learned, and it's not easily learned in the abstract. One learns to worship by being part of a worshiping community. But worship that is heavily word oriented is not really very inclusive. It presents obstacles to the cognitively impaired, whether a developmentally disabled person or an adult afflicted with some form of senile dementia. And it's not very inclusive of children, no matter how carefully those worship kits are put together. But the sacraments can be inclusive of all these people. And children are particularly included when the form of celebration involves getting up and moving toward the Table.

But it's not only the cognitively impaired or children who benefit from worship in which preaching is regularly and frequently set next to sacramental worship. In an essay in *The Christian Century*, Miroslav Volf described his experience when he and his family had moved to a new community. Visiting one church after another, he felt starved for spiritual nourishment.

> High view of the ministry of the Word and pronounced free church sensibilities notwithstanding, I finally caved in. I sought refuge from bad preaching in the celebration of the Eucharist. . . . Dissatisfied with ministers who live by their own wisdom, I turned to the Eucharist.[5]

It's not true, of course, that the Eucharist is merely some kind of compensation for consistent failures in preaching, although for those who seek a vital ministry of the Word in vain, it may very well prove to be a refuge. When Book and Meal, Word and sacrament call and respond to each other, sing to one another antiphonally, each becomes stronger, truer to itself. Frequent celebration of the Eucharist is no excuse for careless preaching, and extraordinarily fine preaching is no excuse for neglect of the Eucharist.

PRIMARY THEOLOGY

Over the years it's become apparent that for many pastors in mainline churches, worship holds little interest except as a vehicle for preaching. So, what does it matter in the long run? Why make such a fuss over details? After all, the heart and core of the faith is in its doctrine, isn't it? In the ancient creeds, the Reformation confessions, the new catechisms? Or in learning biblical content? Or in our mission—getting straight what we need to do to press this world toward something at least resembling God's new creation? So, why does it matter what form the liturgy takes? It may be useful in gathering people to hear the sermon, or pumping them up to do what they ought to do. But apart from that, why does it matter what we do as long as it's interesting enough to bring in a congregation?

I would argue that there is something of vital importance about what we do in the Sunday assembly. The reason it's important is that it's in our worship where we do our primary theology. The official compendia of denominational doctrine will not directly influence most people. Most will never do any basic theological study. Many will not even be exposed much to Scripture on their own. The vast majority will learn their theology from their experiences of worship.

Will anyone who cares about the faith dispute the fact that theology matters? It doesn't matter, certainly, to most people to learn academic theology. A committed layperson won't find it essential to be able to summarize the differences between Paul Tillich and Karl Barth, or between Sally McFague and George Lindbeck. But theology as a way of incorporating, internalizing, and then communicating the nature of our hope certainly does matter. Our hope, rooted in the triune God, is set against what Lesslie Newbigin calls "the reigning plausibility structure."[6] The reigning plausibility structure refers to the way people who live in our time and in our culture perceive reality. Living within the plausibility structure, we are not likely to be able to see it objectively or recognize its power to shape the way we perceive things. The plausibility structure that reigns in North American and European culture has no role for God, unless as a bit player who makes an occasional cameo appearance. The reigning plausibility structure is enormously powerful, but it can be questioned. Our theology does exactly that. For most Christian people, the power of an alternative vision of reality manifests itself in worship, where Scripture and meal, supported by prayer and song, reframe the world as God's world, redeemed and to be redeemed in Christ.

One can see best how theology matters, I suppose, when looking at the damage bad theology can do. Some in our churches have experienced the kind of theology based on threats of hellfire and damnation. Some have been at least tempted to buy a theology based on the gospel of wealth. "Love God and get rich! You know God wants you to have that Mercedes!" Churches that make no distinction between gospel and nation, or gospel and tribe, or gospel and class, propagate a flawed theology.

Maybe it's harder for us to notice the effects of *good* theology, but it has an effect, too. In one of Charles Schultz's *Peanuts* comic strips, Linus and Lucy are looking out the window as the rain pours down in torrents. Lucy says, "Boy, look at it rain. What if it floods the whole world?" Linus replies, "It will never do that. In the ninth chapter of Genesis, God promised Noah that would never happen again, and the sign of the promise is the rainbow." Lucy, a huge smile on her face, says, "You've taken a great load off my mind." Linus answers, "Sound theology has a way of doing that!"[7]

Theology matters not just in some abstract way, not just for the sake of being on the right side in an argument, not just for having figured out the rules well enough to avoid hell and get your ticket to heaven punched. Theology matters because it shapes our discipleship, and because it shapes the life of the church, and because it shapes the kinds of mission we do. Theology matters because it seasons our disposition, positions us in the world and in the world to come, and directs us where to invest our hope. Theology matters because it properly orients us to God and our neighbor. It matters because it clears a space to be open to God in a world that, for all practical purposes, has shut God out. Sound theology really does take a load off the mind!

Theology matters not just to the academy and not just to ministers, but to the whole church and to everyone who comes within the orbit of the church and its mission. And because theology matters, the means we use to communicate that theology matter. And guess what? Human beings aren't just walking intellects. We are whole persons who are formed not only by what we hear but also by what we experience—what we touch, what we feel, what we smell, what we eat, what we say, what we sing, what we do, how we move. The church "traditions" its gospel—hands on its gospel—in its worship. Not just in that part of worship expressed in words, but in the whole gestalt of worship. And that's why it matters what we do there.

When I advocate recovering the deep tradition, the tradition of Word and sacrament, sacrament and Word, I'm not arguing that some worship is valid and other worship not. It's not as though we need to satisfy some legal requirement. I'm not saying that we have to find and re-create the pattern of what some have called "the primitive church," nor that we have to re-create Calvin's way, or Luther's, or Wesley's. What I am saying is that worship is primary theology. And primary theology is best served by making use of those resources of which the earliest Christians already had some experience, resources that are themselves rooted in the ministry of Jesus: Word and sacrament—or Book, Bath, Meal, and attentiveness to the poor, as Lathrop describes the central things. Primary theology is best served when it's rooted not in lessons to be learned, but in meeting the risen Lord.

CHRIST MEMORIAL

Driving west on I-70 in May, I saw a sign identifying a church as Christ Memorial Baptist Church. What's the primary theology that led to naming a church Christ Memorial? In Omaha, there's a Luther Memorial Church and a Calvin Memorial Church. In Richmond, there's a Wesley Memorial Church. But a Christ Memorial Church? The presumption would seem to be that Christ is dead and gone. I suspect that there are not just a few people in mainline pews on Sunday morning who presume that Christ is the classic religious teacher, the badly treated hero and martyr now dead and gone but whose lessons are still available to us. And how did they acquire such a point of view? From many sources, no doubt; some of them from the surrounding culture. But also, unfortunately and not infrequently, from the primary theology acquired in the Sunday morning assembly. And a theology of a God imprisoned in the past is a faulty theology.

When the Puritans launched their attempt to reform worship in England, they tended to go back to the Bible to try to find a text to justify every little thing. Was it permitted to kneel for Communion? What does the Bible say? Was it permitted to wear the surplice? What does the Bible say? Was it permitted for the congregation to say the Nicene Creed? What does the Bible say? Is it permitted to pray the Lord's Prayer, or is that just a model for our edification? What does the Bible say?

The search for a text to justify every little movement in worship can easily lead to absurdity. Does the Bible permit sound-amplification systems? Does Scripture allow the preacher to step outside the pulpit? That's not the kind of "primary theology" I have in mind.

THE BIBLE AND WORSHIP

The Bible is not a service book or a list of rules related to particular orders of service. But that doesn't mean that Scripture has nothing to say about worship. In fact, it may say rather more than we've been attentive to. Gordon Lathrop points out that all four Gospels

> follow exactly the same shape: baptism, narratives, meal and passion, resurrection and sending. . . . Such a list is, in exactly this order, recognizable to us as the emerging shape of the Christian Sunday meeting.[8]

The Bible may speak about worship without announcing what it's doing. Take, for example, the story about the walk to Emmaus, in Luke 24. This is a wonderful story that tells something about the Lucan community's ways of worship and its experience in worship. It's not, as one post-Reformation preacher imagined, about the benefits of healthful walks in the country! You know how it goes. Two persons, members of the wider circle of disciples, are walking from Jerusalem to Emmaus on Easter afternoon. As they walk, they're discussing the things that have happened in the past few days, including Jesus' crucifixion and rumors that he'd been seen alive. They're joined by a stranger. The reader knows who the stranger is. Luke tells us it's Jesus. But the two disciples didn't recognize him. He joined their discussion, quoting from Hebrew Scripture as a way of interpreting what's happened. They reached a village near their destination, and the two invited Jesus to have a meal with them. While they were at table, Jesus "took bread, blessed and broke it, and gave it to them."

You might notice that there's a certain similarity between this account and the story of the feeding of the five thousand. Here's how Luke describes the beginning of that meal: "And taking the five loaves and the two fish, he looked up to heaven, and blessed and broke them, and gave them to the disciples to set before the crowd" (Luke 9:16). Notice the verbs that occur in the two accounts: took (or taking), blessed, broke, gave. There's still another similarity in Luke's account of the Last Supper. "Then he took a loaf of bread, and when he had given thanks, he broke it and gave it to them" (Luke 22:19). Took, gave thanks, broke, gave. The use of these verbs in that particular sequence is not an accident. Luke is linking these three meals—one during Jesus' ministry, another at the crisis-point near the end of his ministry, and the other after the crucifixion and resurrection. Took, gave thanks, broke, gave. In the Emmaus story, the giving of the blessed and broken bread is followed by something remarkable. "Then their eyes were opened, and they recognized him" (Luke 24:31).

Luke has a point to make here, and the point comes from the primary theology of the community among whom he worshiped. The point is that, after the resurrection, the taking, blessing, breaking, and giving of the bread among Jesus' disciples is somehow joined to their experience of the presence of the risen Lord.

The disciples ran to report to the eleven: "Then they told what had happened on the road, and how he had been made known to them in the breaking of the bread" (Luke 24:35). The Eucharist, the Lord's Supper, was important to the Lucan community. In case the reader misses it, Luke adds the story of the risen Jesus eating a piece of broiled fish in their presence (Luke 24:41–43). In John 21, that very different Gospel makes a similar point when Jesus, at first unrecognized, appears on the shore of the Sea of Galilee. After the crucifixion, the disciples had gone back to fishing. The story ends with a meal eaten on the beach, the risen Lord in the midst of the disciples.

But there's more to the Emmaus road story that Luke told. After Jesus had vanished from their sight, the disciples said to each other, "Were not our hearts burning within us while he was talking to us on the road, while he was opening the scriptures to us?" (Luke 24:32). This represents another facet of the worship life of Luke's community. Jesus touches the believers as he opens up the Scriptures for them. The same Jesus who was disclosed at the Table had earlier been revealed in the opening of the Scriptures.

In the worship life of the early community we already see the outlines of Word and sacrament—in this case, Book and Meal. One of the most noteworthy things about Word and sacrament as Luke's community experiences them is that both are portrayed in sacramental terms, preaching as well as the Lord's Supper. Scripture isn't just *about* Jesus. Jesus himself is active in the process of opening the Scriptures to us. His presence is sensed in those terms dear to the hearts of the Wesleys—experienced as the heart "strangely warmed," burning within us. And in the breaking of bread, the church doesn't just engage in an audiovisual stimulus to the memory. It expects that our eyes will be opened and that we will recognize Christ in our midst. Powerful things, Word and sacrament, primary theology.

EUCHARIST AS NEXUS
OF PAST, PRESENT, AND FUTURE

It's also worth noting that this experience of the sacrament is not focused exclusively on Jesus' suffering and death, or on our need for repentance. Luke has linked three quite different meals. One is that open-air picnic that serves as a foretaste of the messianic banquet, the same meal anticipated on another occasion when Jesus described it in these words: "Then people will come from east and west, from north and south, and will eat in the kingdom of God" (Luke 13:29). Another meal occasion is the Last Supper, in which there is a sense of foreboding and anxiety. But the other meals of which Luke and John speak are postresurrection meals. Certainly Luke and his community understood the Lord's Supper not only in terms of loss, and death, and suffering, and penitence, but also in terms of rejoicing, eating and drinking with the risen Lord, and also as a joyful and expectant anticipation of the messianic banquet in the kingdom of heaven.

This makes a difference to us. We Protestants imported into our own services of Holy Communion the somber, penitential caste of the late medieval Mass. Although this rather grim piety is not indigenous to Protestantism, it was perpetuated in most Protestant traditions. One example of it is the Scottish preparatory services that preceded every celebration of the Lord's Supper by several days to provide times of introspection and confession. The multiple sermons preceding the great outdoor Scottish Communions became the prototype for the American camp meeting, with its emphasis on sin and repentance. The churches have not yet entirely shaken this powerful association of the Lord's Supper with a grim piety.

It wasn't until after the mid-twentieth century that newer Protestant service books and liturgical guides finally sought to correct this view of the Lord's Supper as a kind of replay of the Last Supper. One example is the 1961 *Directory for Worship*, drafted for the former United Presbyterian Church U.S.A. by Robert McAfee Brown. It reads, "The promise of Christ's presence in the midst of those who receive this sacrament witnesses to the reality of his resurrection from the dead and is a foretaste of eternal fellowship with him."[9] The themes of resurrection and anticipation of the messianic banquet are echoed in the newer service books of all the historic Protestant denominations. Those who notice this, and shape their Communion celebrations in accordance with it, find that, though it's tough going sometimes, it's possible to shift from "funeral for Jesus" to eating and drinking with the risen Lord. When the shift is made to incorporate resurrection and eschatological hope alongside "remembering the Lord's death," the psychological resistance to frequent Communion can begin to be overcome.

RESHAPING TRADITIONS

Early in my ministry I was pastor of a young congregation, a new-church development. The congregation was only four years old when I became the first pastor to serve it full-time. There were few traditions, and on many occasions I had the opportunity to try to shape traditions. What should we do, for example, on Christmas Eve? It was decided that we would celebrate the Lord's Supper at the Christmas Eve service. We decided also that we would not serve Communion in the pews. This was no radical move, because there had been no Christmas Eve service before my arrival, and because people are more willing to try something new in extraordinary services than on Sunday mornings, for the most part. We served Communion by inviting people to come in groups to stand in a complete circle around the Communion table in the chancel. We passed the bread and the cup around the circle, each serving their neighbor.

When all in the circle had been served, the minister took the hand of the person next to him and extended the peace of Christ. Each in turn took their neighbor by the hand, and one by one each offered the peace of Christ until it had passed completely around the circle and back to the minister. Not particularly unusual, is it? But here's something I noticed: Spouses taking each other by the hand and extending the peace of Christ to each other as the whole congregation was silent. Parents extending the peace of Christ to their children. Grandparents to grandchildren. People present every Sunday to people present only on Christmas Eve.

The look in people's eyes told me that something really important was going on there. In that configuration I could see more clearly that the Eucharist is powerful. No doubt that power is present when church officers take the bread and cup to the pews. But I could see it with far more clarity in that setting where the Eucharist was made larger, where peace and reconciliation in families and among neighbors and strangers was so movingly acted out as an integral part of the sacrament.

One thing I discovered in those occasions was that the church already has in the treasury of its tradition marvelous resources for the cure of souls. Before we try to invent resources heretofore unknown, we might be well advised to visit that treasury, that dusty storehouse. Even when we've lost track of precious things stored away there, they still belong to us. It's not too late to pull them out and dust them off and put them to use. New generations will find that the Holy Spirit who breathed life into those precious things in the first place will breathe life into them again.

In two congregations I've served, we introduced a new service with a full sermon and weekly Eucharist. In this era, many congregations that once gave up one of their Sunday services are now considering adding a service. And some churches that have never had more than one service are mulling over the possibility of creating a new one, either earlier on Sunday morning or on Saturday evening. Congregations might imagine that a second service should resemble a seeker service, like Willow Creek's, or at least that it should be based on a completely different musical idiom. Perhaps the secret of its success would be to puncture every conceivable pomposity and resemble the *Oprah Winfrey Show* or one of its lookalikes.

But another possibility ought to be considered—the possibility of creating a service that turns equally around Word and sacrament, every week. It need not be a duplicate of the somber Communion services that may be the experience of the eleven o'clock congregation. It could be very much alive with the sense of meeting the risen Lord. Biblical preaching would anchor such a service in the gospel story. The Eucharist could make clear that this whole service is about presence and about meeting, something entirely different than a pep rally or a talk show or adult education or fulfilling some onerous obligation. The music may be more eclectic than the standard eleven o'clock service. The instrumentation may branch out to include instruments along with the organ, or instead of it. The service may rely more on action and somewhat less on words. There may be less use of written texts in the service itself; less reading from printed orders of service and more song; more verbal than printed cues. The congregation may move more than has been customary, and their active participation may be more intentionally solicited. The manner of celebrating such a service may vary enormously, but it is the synergy of Book and Meal, Word and sacrament, that gives energy to it.

The Eucharist, which has been made smaller among us, can be made larger. And making it larger more clearly reveals the magnificence of the God who's visited us in Christ. When the Eucharist is made larger, the ministry of the Word may grow into its proper largeness as well. The sacraments, rightly understood, always bear witness to good news. The Bible and the proclamation of the Scriptures, rightly understood, always bear witness to good news. This is true even when the biblical text confronts us with what seems like bad news. In worship that makes larger both Word and sacrament, the primary theology is a theology of good news, and that good news is first of all the resurrection of the crucified Lord.

I think we might find that it's possible to reframe the quotation from Howard Hageman to sound more like this: "If the church that honors the Word discovers the power of the sacrament, is it not also true that the church that honors the sacrament discovers the power of the Word?"

Chapter 6

What Will the Future Bring?

A few years ago I read an article in a denominational journal by some-one who predicted that by about the year 2030, the last Presbyterian could turn out the lights. I doubt it. Many prognosticators try to pre-dict the future by imagining the extension and expansion of current trends. Maybe some things can be predicted that way, but hardly any-thing that has to do with human beings can be so easily forecast. Even as late as the mid-'80s, people who taught Soviet studies didn't pre-dict the fall of the Iron Curtain or the abrupt end of the U.S.S.R. His-tory is a complex phenomenon, full of unpredictables. Hidden factors are at work that alter the equation.

In the early '70s, a young man asked me what I thought the future of the church looked like. The image I conjured up for him was noth-ing more than an amplification of conventionally trendy speculation of the time—house churches, small, covenanted communities entirely unlike the institutional church as we knew it then and know it now. When we attempt to see the future, most of us see what's in fashion today magnified a hundred times. But the truth is, we really don't know what the future will hold, and that's true for the church in general and for its worship life in particular.

Some have predicted that Willow Creek and seeker services and so-called "contemporary worship" are the wave of the future. I suspect that they will have a *place* in the future, but won't be the *wave* of the future. Willow Creek, the seeker service, much of what's called contemporary worship, these are all deeply rooted in American church history. They are a culturally updated form of the camp meeting and the tent revival. Because they're so deeply rooted in American populism, they're not likely ever to disappear. In fact, they've always been with us in one form or another and will continue to be. But today's grand experiments will recede to the margins again, at least for a while, until they reappear in another era in still other forms.

When I began my ministry, the historic churches of the mainline had begun to experience the rising influence of the twentieth-century liturgical renaissance. I imagined that by the close of my ministry, a service oriented around Word and table would have become the norm in American Protestantism. The liturgical renewal has had enormous impact, but it's not the norm, and I'm not sure that it ever will be.

In those early days, I could imagine the worship of the various Christian churches growing closer and closer, until one could scarcely distinguish one denomination's service from another. There has, in fact, been convergence. The texts of the service books in the mainline denominations and in the Roman Catholic Church could probably be switched around without many people noticing as long as local protocols weren't violated. But it's apparent to me now that there will never be just one form of worship common to all churches.

DIVERSITY

The future of Christian worship is likely to remain diverse. At the dawn of the twentieth century, when among both Roman Catholics and Protestants in Europe and the United States the first faint glimmerings of liturgical renewal began, no one would have predicted the rise and spread of Pentecostalism. And yet, Pentecostalism has grown and is growing all around the world. Is Pentecostalism the wave of the future? Or will it die out? Or might it be transformed by experience? Like nearly every other movement in the church, Pentecostalism has drawn attention to things that deserved attention but didn't get it. In this case, it brought attention to the Holy Spirit's work in the church. There's something vital there. Who can predict what kinds of synergy are at work in, between, and among traditions? What kind of chemistry might be at work between Pentecostalism and the historic churches? And yet, I don't think that Pentecostalism in and of itself will be the only wave of the future.

Will it be Eastern Orthodoxy? Orthodoxy is at last beginning to make itself at home in the American environment. It attracts a good many converts from Protestantism as well as from Roman Catholicism. A richness is there that well deserves attention. Yet, I don't think it will sweep away the other churches.

Will Roman Catholicism finally triumph? I suspect that it may certainly more and more resemble the default setting for American Christianity, taking the place historically claimed by Protestant churches. Yet it has internal weaknesses and contradictions that will prevent it from sweeping the field.

Will the wave of the future be 1950s-style generic Protestant worship? I think that's the least likely to survive. Least likely, because it's so tied to the presumptions of the Enlightenment, which are fast fading.

WHAT CONSERVATIVES
AND LIBERALS HAVE IN COMMON

We're truly living in an in-between time. The Enlightenment provided most mainline Protestants and their pastors (along with everyone else) with a framework for understanding the world. Even those who've never heard of the Enlightenment have been decisively shaped by its presumptions. The Enlightenment saw the world in terms of the old Newtonian physics. It was a closed system, a giant machine, a series of causes and effects that allowed no room for God. The Enlightenment world is a world where everything is rational, and—sooner or later—understandable. It's a world with a low tolerance for ambiguity and for paradox.

The Enlightenment worldview has shaped both ends of the Protestant spectrum, the very conservative end and the very liberal end. Conservative and liberal alike have accepted the terms laid down by the Enlightenment. Each is literalistic in its own way. The fundamentalists use strained arguments to justify every line in the Bible as literally true. Those on the far left strain out everything in Scripture that doesn't fit the model of Enlightenment rationality—or, if not strain it out, strain to recast it in terms they imagine to be reasonable. For example, it's not uncommon to hear preachers suggest that one can understand the gospel stories of the feeding of the five thousand as a miracle of sharing, in which the crowd was shamed by the example of the generosity of the boy with five loaves and two fish. Moved by his offering, according to some commentators, the people brought out of hiding the food they had been carrying with them for their exclusive use. Or one may find a commentary that ponders whether the four jars of water the prophet Elijah poured on the wood, to which God set fire, might in fact have been kerosene (1 Kgs. 18:33). The Enlightenment worldview needs to explain everything, as though the important agenda were to verify an historical record rather than listen for a Word that may overflow the historical record. By and large, the Enlightenment has no use for mystery, and sees it only as obfuscation.

Yet, the world of the Enlightenment has already begun to slip away. I'm not sure that the curriculum taught in public schools knows yet that the Enlightenment world is on the way out. Its presumptions still grip a lot of people. But that's precisely one source of the tension and dis-ease we feel in society and in the church. We have begun to be influenced by a post-Enlightenment point of view, and some more influenced by it than others. Most of us feel personally torn, and every group is torn, because we are being pulled simultaneously in two directions. One, the familiar direction of the world that held so firm fifty or seventy-five years ago; the other the direction of what some have labeled as postmodern. The worship of the 1950s belongs to the Enlightenment world, whether that worship stems from the left or right wing of American Protestantism. And much that's labeled seeker or contemporary worship also belongs to the Enlightenment world. That's why I don't predict a rosy future for either one.

THE FADING
OF THE ENLIGHTENMENT-SHAPED WORLD

What's happened to cause the Enlightenment worldview to fade and another to begin to emerge? What's happened is quantum physics.[1] I don't understand quantum physics and can't possibly explain anything about it, but I do know that it has displaced the old Newtonian model. It has discredited the conventional mechanistic model of the universe and made much more room for variables—perhaps even chance—in the workings of things. Neither the subatomic world nor the macrocosmic world conforms to the patterns that seem so apparent in our middle-sized world. Quantum theory has put an end to the fantasy that, at bottom, reality is like a machine whose workings become apparent when we take it apart. Newtonian physics contributed to the tendency of the Enlightenment to suggest that science deals with fact while religion deals with private opinion.[2] Misreading the nature of scientific investigation, with an optimistic assessment of the objectivity of human reason, the Newtonian model contributed to the kind of rationalism that has often disfigured our theology and our worship.

Contemporary students of physics have introduced a new way of looking at how people know things, based in part on their own discoveries as they have attempted to see how the world works on a subatomic level. Barbara Brown Taylor summarizes the revolution in physics when she writes,

> In a discovery that upsets all our previous notions of space and time, we have found out that two particles separated by whole galaxies "know" what each other is doing. Change the spin on one and the other reverses its spin wherever it is—instantaneously—using some form of communication that is faster than light. . . . Mystery is once again loose in the cosmos. With the development of quantum physics, we discovered a subatomic world that did not behave the way Newton said it should. It was impossible to pin down, with waves turning into particles and particles into waves. What had mass one moment was pure energy the next, and none of it was predictable. The very act of observing a particle changed its behavior, which destroyed the whole notion of scientific objectivity. A scientist could not stand outside the world to watch it. The same particles that were busy responding to each other responded to the watcher as well, revealing a world that was not made up of manageable things but of constantly changing relationships.[3]

This post-Enlightenment view of the world has not turned its back on rationality. It doesn't propose to replace rationality with irrationality. Every system of thought, whether religious or scientific, is rational because it reasons from given premises. What's in dispute are the basic premises, the beginning points from which we reason. The

Christian faith begins with the conviction of God's self-disclosure in Jesus Christ, taking that as key to understanding the true nature of things. True rationality, from that point of view, is relational. In other words, rationality doesn't follow a kind of mathematical or geometrical model. The world is evolutionary, dynamic, and in process of becoming. We know, not because we keep ourselves at a distance from what's to be known, but by participating in the thing known. We know by becoming engaged rather than disengaged. We know more profoundly when we know in a kind of holistic way rather than when we propose to take things apart. And what we know in that holistic way can never be completely reduced to words.

A necessary ingredient to this kind of knowing—and I'm not just talking about religious ways of knowing, but also of the way that scientists come to know things—is imagination. Imagination, in this case, doesn't mean making things up. It refers rather to the capacity to visualize possibilities other than the customary ones, the ones taken for granted. Imagination enables us to see things as they might be, rather than as we have been accustomed to seeing them. I suppose there's an element of intuitiveness in this way of defining the word *imagination*. Now, of course, imagination can mislead, or send us down a blind alley. But imagination can also break out of the conventional and open vast new landscapes. Imagination thrives on community and feeds on metaphor. I can't tell you how many times in congregations I've served or in the classroom an individual has offered an insight that has opened my eyes to something I'd never seen before. In encountering a biblical text, or scrutinizing the way one text relates to another, someone looking at it with fresh eyes sees it in an imaginative way, not employing a step-by-step reasoning process, but an insightful breakthrough. This is not significantly different than the way scientific breakthroughs occur.[4]

TORN BETWEEN TWO WORLDS

This is, I recognize, an all-too-sketchy outline of what amounts to nothing less than a full-scale revolution, which is even now thrusting us into a new era as different from the Enlightenment as the Enlightenment was from premodern times. Now we're torn, because we have feet in the old camp and in the new. We've begun to perceive and to assimilate the new even when we don't know why. It's in the air around us, just as the Enlightenment was, and still is, in the air around us. A time will come, however, when the Enlightenment will lose its hold and people won't be torn between one worldview and another. The Enlightenment has had a long run. We're either unlucky to be caught in between eras, or lucky to be present at the dawning of a new one. Take your choice!

From my point of view, the new, postmodern era has some real positives. In some ways, it's more compatible with a biblical way of thinking than is the Enlightenment worldview. The "modern" or "Enlightenment" worldview presumed that everything can be investigated and known, and by being known, presumably mastered. If there's room for God in that worldview, it's only a trivial God. As Merold Westphal has written in a recent issue of *Perspectives*, "This God evokes neither awe nor music and dance."[5]

The God of the Bible is mystery, known in faith, yes, but never entirely comprehended. The Bible is rich with symbol and metaphor. It kindles the imagination, opens up a broader world, gives us glimpses of reality through God's eyes. It seems to me that encountering something whole, rather than disengaging from the whole, taking it apart into its separate pieces, is a biblical way of knowing. This way of knowing is compatible with a rich sacramental life. In the sacraments we are engaged holistically. At font and table, we have an appointment with God and God's people, those who lived in the past, those living yet, and those yet to be born. The sacraments appeal to the whole person, not just the intellect, not just the emotions, not just the senses. It's not by accident, I think, that this sensual way of knowing has emerged out of the ministry of Jesus and the life of the community.

Jane Vann has written, "In worship we find a coming together of metaphor, participatory knowing, and revelation."[6] The symbols in worship participate in the reality they represent. As we encounter them, chew on them, inwardly digest them, we also participate in that re-presented reality. We don't leave our intellects behind, but neither do we isolate our intellects from our whole personhood. In faith, we affirm that in symbol and metaphor, in Scripture, preaching, and sacrament, God reveals Godself to God's people.

If this is true, then ways of worship shaped by Enlightenment rationalism will not be the wave of the future. Like nearly everything else, they will persist, commanding some kind of loyal constituency, but they won't be tomorrow's success story. Which means that, whether described as traditional or contemporary, worship that flattens out metaphor and rationalizes it, worship that looks down its nose on the sacraments, worship that flattens out or minimizes Scripture, and worship that presumes the worshipers will remain impassive and immobile is yesterday's success story, but not tomorrow's.

One reason that we are so in-between, so uncertain, pulled this way and that, is that some of our constituency are untouched by postmodern sensibilities, or touched only enough to be troubled by them. Others have been profoundly influenced by them. Those who are untouched—or who wish they were—hold on to the ways of worship they've known, rooted in an Enlightenment worldview. Those who relate more nearly to the postmodern era know that Enlightenment-shaped worship doesn't work for them but they don't know why not, and they don't know what will. So we flounder, adjusting the music, dressing down, using new technologies. While the novelty may appeal to some, and others may feel some temporary relief from their puzzling sense of alienation, we run the risk of missing the boat. The newly popular ways, the so-called contemporary ways, don't necessarily challenge the Enlightenment worldview. More often than not, they are anything but contemporary. They're the last gasp of a world in the process of passing away.

THE CONTEMPORARY
IS TRADITIONAL AFTER ALL

Dean Inge has said, "He who weds the spirit of the age soon finds himself widowed." I think that's true in any era. It's certainly true in our own, where the spirit of the age is stretched between two vastly different worldviews, one passing, one emerging. Don't get me wrong. I think the crisis is sufficient that it's certainly worth coloring outside the lines, working outside the conventional parameters, pushing the envelope. But many of the changes associated with "contemporary" worship are superficial when it comes right down to it, as much as they may seem radical to traditionalists. I would be very surprised if they had a long shelf life.

Worship of any kind seems barely compatible with the survival skills people need in contemporary culture. In order to survive in our society, we learn all the skills of independent individualism. We learn how to compete effectively, how to make and discard friends and acquaintances, how to move from job to job, from house to house, from community to community, and even from family to family as though nothing and no one had any real hold on us. We learn these survival skills in varying degrees. And to the extent that they form our consciousness and shape our behavior, they become profoundly antithetical to the values of the gospel, which the church's worship, and particularly its sacramental life, represents.

National Public Radio broadcast an interview with Robert Putnam, the author of the book *Bowling Alone: The Collapse and Revival of American Community*.[7] He cited statistics to prove that the trends he'd spotted in the book are increasing. Fewer and fewer people are joining any kind of group. Associations like the PTA have declined by 40 to 50 percent. And it's not just organized groups. There's been a 60 percent decline in people going on picnics; a 40 percent decline in people visiting bars; and even a 30 percent decline in people having dinner with their own family. People watch *Friends* on TV, but they don't have friends. The more television folks watch, the less likely they are to join anything. Churches do well to hold the loyalties of as many people as they do.

One commentator notes that

> It is not difficult to see that a major source of contemporary alienation from our liturgy lies in the fact that the attitudes we need to survive in our culture are profoundly at odds with the attitudes presupposed and fostered by our liturgical traditions.[8]

Radical individualism and personal autonomy may proceed out of an Enlightenment sensibility, but because they're reinforced by our economic system, and because they offer material rewards, they have a powerful hold. It appears that people can be modern and postmodern at the same time. The qualities of individualism and autonomy derived from and typical of the modern period have been cut loose from their Enlightenment moorings and become self-justifying and self-sustaining. Some churches have identified these modern qualities and resolved to capitalize on them. These are the churches that preach the gospel of success. "God wants you to be rich, God wants you to be successful, God wants you to realize your dreams, to get that promotion, to beat out the competition." Some of these churches draw big crowds.

Radical individualism and the search for personal autonomy are likely to persist even after the Enlightenment sensibility has further waned. But churches would do better to become self-consciously countercultural at this point. Not for the sake of drawing a crowd, because counterculturalism may not draw crowds, but countercultural in the sense of being true to the gospel that pulls us into relationship with God and one another and with neighbors near and far, and the whole communion of saints. What use is numerical success if we end up being something we weren't meant to be? Weren't called to be? Aren't commissioned and empowered to be?

DOMESTICATED OR COUNTERCULTURAL?

A layperson active in a church in a large Canadian city claims that it is not uncommon for pastors to report losing members who have become converts to Islam, which has become a significant presence in that city. Since the events of September 11, 2001, there have been newspaper accounts of similar coversions in the United States not only among African Americans but also among Latinos and Anglos. The evidence is anecdotal, and there is no evidence of a moving tide. But even if the numbers are small, they provoke us to ask why mainstream Christians would be attracted to Islam. One possible explanation is that, in North America, Islam is distinctly different from the common culture. Could it be that some thoughtful people understand that the conventional culture is not adequate to put us in touch with deeper things? That if one is seeking for a true path, it will probably require looking beyond what everybody takes for granted? Unfortunately, the church seems very frequently to reflect and affirm the surrounding culture. It may be, of course, that there are always some folks in search of the exotic. But it may also be that a compelling Christianity will always exist in some tension with its host culture.

The pursuit of the church's countercultural mission in a postmodern way will certainly include, I think, turning to a deeper, richer, sacramental, and metaphoric worship, as well as a more profound attentiveness to the poor. This worship will include preaching that is sacramental, metaphoric, and symbolic as well as discursive. The metaphoric and symbolic will affect the way we pray as well as the ways we celebrate the sacraments themselves. The worshiping assembly will understand itself more clearly as a royal priesthood, interceding on behalf of the vulnerable, the voiceless, the faithless, the bewildered, and the harried. I suspect that worship which is richer in these ways may look quite different from place to place and time to time. It won't be just a replay of what worked in Geneva or Wittenberg in the sixteenth century, or Rome in the twelfth century, or Antioch in the second. It won't be all of us reading off the same page. But it will be informed by the deep tradition, which in some ways is remarkably similar to the emerging post-Enlightenment worldview.

Will it create a mass movement back to church? Who can say? In a *Bowling Alone* culture, who can predict the course of anything that challenges that culture? In a culture in which prosperity has become linked to individualism and personal autonomy, who knows which forces will prevail? But worship that takes seriously the deep tradition of gospel and church will still be there when worship shaped by the Enlightenment, whether traditional or contemporary, has been abandoned.

So, listening carefully to Dean Inge's warning, the caution is not to embrace too wholeheartedly whatever trends seem to be winners at the moment. While not always true, very often the current experiments have introduced only cosmetic changes in worship. Their special appeal is in having apparently overturned worship of the parental generation, the religious establishment of another age. Much of its attractiveness is found in its upbeat quality and its power to amuse, to keep boredom at bay for an hour or so. But, as Douglas John Hall has said,

> I believe I am not mistaken in saying that Christianity is a demanding and serious religion. When it is delivered as easy and amusing, it is *another kind of religion altogether.*[9]

CONTINUITIES AND DISCONTINUITIES

There are always continuities in history. People are people, whatever the surrounding culture and the changing sensibilities. Some constants remain. Nevertheless, historians have argued over whether there is such a thing as "national character"—for example, the old clichés that presume that Germans are highly organized and Italians are great lovers. And theologians have argued over whether such a thing as "human nature" exists. The arguments arise from the fact that, while human characteristics persist across time and cultures, people are also apparently profoundly influenced by their cultural environments. Despite continuities, one can also find significant discontinuities in the human family. The issue has been framed in another way: Which is more influential, nature or nurture? Researchers have explored that question in studies of identical twins.

These are important questions when we think about the future of worship. Because of "nature"—that is, our common humanity—we are not entirely different from the people of biblical times or the early centuries of the church or the Reformation. And yet, because of "nurture"—cultural influences—we do experience the world differently, in some ways, than they did. We can presume that people continue to hunger for God, to long for some taste of the eternal in the midst of the temporal. We can suppose that people are programmed to hope, and to look for some place or someone where they can safely and confidently invest their hope. There's the continuity. But it's also safe to presume that worship which served those interests in one era may be dysfunctional in another.

A few years ago, William Strauss and Neil Howe wrote a book called *Generations: The History of America's Future, 1584 to 2069.*[10] Strauss and Howe use an historical analysis to describe the processes of change from generation to generation. They argue that over the course of American history, there has been a cyclic pattern by which one generational type follows another in a roughly predictable course. The argument is fairly simple. Each generation bounces off its experience with the parental generation. It doesn't simply reproduce the values of the parental generation, but engages in a process of correcting, and sometimes overcorrecting, what it perceives to have been a fault in the parental generation. For example, a generation that typically resorted to strict methods of childrearing may produce offspring whose commitment is to ease up on their own children. A generation that in childhood experienced the discontinuity of a much-divorced parental generation may approach their own marriages very differently. Strauss and Howe examine how each generation influences the subsequent one, and in this way they have come up with four basic generational types, which seem to recycle one after the other.

Strauss and Howe have their critics, of course. No doubt their analysis contains flaws. But a strength of their argument is that there are at least statistical similarities in generational cohorts that identify them and distinguish them from the statistical profiles of the generational cohorts before and after. All the writing about baby boomers and Generation X is not entirely fictional. Not all boomers are alike, certainly. Nor have they all had the same sort of childhood experience. But statistical studies can identify certain points of view and other characteristics that predominate among that generational group and make them different from, for example, Generation X.

Strauss and Howe's analysis is helpful. They're simply saying that culture influences people, and that people born within a few years of one another will share a common historical experience. One generation remembers the Kennedy assassination to which they were exposed as adults, another recalls it as a childhood memory, and another doesn't remember it at all. There is a generation that was taught some acquaintance or at least respect for classical music, another generation for whom early rock was a cultural revolution, and still another that has never known anything but the popular music of the past decade. Not everyone in any of those generational cohorts is identical, but statistically, each generation can be identified in distinction from other generations.

Strauss and Howe argue that children born between 1981 and 2001 will form a rough generational cohort, and it will be a generation that does not resemble the baby boomers or Generation X. It will, they argue, more nearly resemble what they call the Civic generation, the generation that experienced the Great Depression and World War II. Certainly the historical circumstances of the Civic generation were unique, yet Strauss and Howe would say that that generation's way of meeting the challenges of their time might have been predicted. The Millennial generation—the 1981 to 2001 folks—will certainly not reproduce the Civic generation, but they will resemble them in the way they engage with the world and react to whatever history dishes up.

The Civic generation is one that appreciated the need to take care of things—institutions, governments, civic obligations. If Strauss and Howe are right, the new rising generation will respect institutions and take responsibility for them in ways different from the intervening generations, the boomers and Generation X.

IS TIME ON OUR SIDE?

What does the rise of a generation significantly different from baby boomers and Generation X mean for the church? Does it mean that all will be well? That all we have to do is wait for these folks to reach maturity, at which point they will replace their aging grandparents or great-grandparents in the pews and on the board of trustees? No. We can't automatically lay claim to the rising generation. It will, after all, live in a different historical time than the Civic generation, and besides that, it will be ever distant from the Enlightenment perspective and culture. It does mean that what appeals to the parents—and even the grandparents, in some cases—of the rising generation will not necessarily appeal to the Millennials. In short, don't hitch your hopes on the solutions invented for the boomers, because they will be irrelevant to most of the Millennials. "He who weds the spirit of the age soon finds himself widowed," you will recall.

I think there's little doubt that a child raised, say, at Willow Creek Church will have a different experience than her parents had. A child exposed to "contemporary worship" as the sole diet of worship will have a different experience than his parents. We have no way to know exactly what sort of appetite that might stimulate in a child, or what sorts of revulsions might have been created. The only thing that's clear is that seeker services and most so-called contemporary worship are probably not the formula for the indefinite future.

There is already some evidence that worship designed to appeal to baby boomers (seeker services and many "contemporary" services) does not appeal to their immediate juniors, the so-called Gen-Xers. Members of Generation X (born between 1965 and 1983) "are more likely to attend church on a given Sunday than their parents—42 percent to 34 percent."[11] Some who work closely with members of this generation testify that, unlike their boomer predecessors, they are more likely to be committed members of congregations. Roman Catholic Gen-Xers are "getting into eucharistic devotion, wanting to pray the rosary."[12] While some churches have tried to appeal to baby boomers by watering down the gospel or simply translating it into a plea for social justice, Gen-Xers find that oversimplification unpalatable.

> If this analysis is correct, churches that want to lure Xers should give up their glitzy, poppy entertainment strategies and stick with the elements of tradition. . . . Xers want the substance, not the packaging. . . . Churches that have catered to sociologists' accounts of what Boomers want (comfort) and what they don't want (doctrine) won't ever get Xers into the pews.[13]

BEYOND SURVIVAL

When it comes to worship, it's true that in every generation there are many who are more or less satisfied with worship that doesn't run very deep, and a relative few who will not be satisfied with anything except that which exhibits some depth. There will always be a constituency for the superficial, and a constituency (though probably smaller) with an appetite for the profound.

So what will the future of Christian worship be? It will be many things, some of which we may admire, some of which may horrify. That's not too different from the way things are now. Where should mainline Protestants be? My intuition tells me that we'd better not place our bets on the Enlightenment models. The future of our worship must take seriously the communal, the relational, the metaphorical, the symbolic, the sacramental—and that includes a serious, thoughtful biblical preaching, which, while intelligent and in touch with where people are, is also communal, relational, metaphorical, symbolic, and sacramental.

The worship life of the church is a critical part of determining the future viability of the church, and it will play a crucial role in either handing on or subverting the substance of the faith. However, the church's worship does not take place in isolation. The shape of the twenty-first-century church will be determined by its worship, including preaching that is strong and wise, but worship cannot be separated from the total ministry of a congregation. We cannot neglect pastoral care, whether offered by ordained officers, by parish nurses, or by trained lay caregivers. We cannot neglect the personal spiritual development of members or the groups within congregations that nurture spiritual growth. We cannot neglect decision-making and governing procedures that grow out of the church's faith and devotion more than out of secular management theories. We cannot neglect attention to biblical literacy, to catechesis, to Christian initiation and formation, including adult education and koinonia. We cannot neglect the people who are not members of our church but for whom the gospel will be a good word. Nor can we neglect our calling to be servants in our communities or to tend to our ties with Christians around the world. Worship is central to the life of the church, and indispensable. Into it and out of it flow all these many other commitments.

Should we care if the mainline churches survive or not? I suspect that the more we concern ourselves with survival for its own sake, the more likely we'll be not to survive. Desperation does not lead to good decisions or wise strategies.

"But perfect love casts out fear," we read in the first letter of John (4:18). It may be that the best strategy of all begins with focusing first of all on our love for God and for the gospel of Jesus Christ, and trusting God's love for us. After all, Jesus promised Peter that "the gates of

Hades" would not prevail against his church (Matt. 16:18). Prayerfully, we offer the best stewardship of the apostolic ministry that we're able to offer. We call the church to exercise its appointed work of being a "royal priesthood," not for its own sake, but to be a blessing "to all the families of the earth." What's of value in the church as we know it will survive, and what's no longer of value will not survive, and we will learn to be content with that. For there will certainly continue to be a true church of God, whose food and drink will be the risen Christ, by the power of the Holy Spirit.

Chapter 7

A New Paradigm for Worship

Some church people dismiss so-called "contemporary worship" as misguided from beginning to end. They interpret it as nothing more or less than a sad concession to vulgar tastes. It is, in their view, a reshaping of worship into entertainment, sacrificing integrity to people's insatiable hunger for distraction. Sometimes that may be exactly what it is, but not always. Sometimes, contemporary worship is a church's attempt to answer the protests of people who are loyal to the church but who find its worship deadening. Sometimes, whether well or badly conceived, contemporary worship at least serves as a signal that this congregation cares about those who have been conspicuous by their absence. This attempt to be responsive may be fumbling and inadequate, or, in some cases, remarkably thoughtful.

One who has had the opportunity to be a visitor in mainline congregations will sometimes be wonderfully surprised, and not infrequently terribly dismayed. One such visitor, away from home, sought out a congregation of her denomination one Sunday not too long ago. She found one not far from her hotel, and was pleased to note in the yellow pages that this church offered three services on Sunday morning. She arrived for the first service, and sat quietly in the sanctuary to get her bearings. It was a lovely building, though somewhat intimidating. Made of stone, it had been designed in a turn-of-the-last-century neo-Gothic style, with a high pulpit. The choir was squeezed into a loft above and behind the pulpit, in a space designed for a paid double-quartet. Above the loft and at the visual center of the sanctuary was the organ case with its exposed pipes. The Communion table and font were out of the line of most of the congregation's sight, and invisible when the people were standing. There was some stained glass in the nave, not particularly remarkable, but most of the windows were finished with plain, opaque glass. The lighting in the sanctuary couldn't overcome the grayness of the stone or the dimness of the windows, and the overall effect was of a cold light. The bulletin that an usher had placed in her hand outlined an order of service not very different from the one to which she was accustomed at home.

The choir sang a complicated Latin anthem perfectly. The organ was lovely. The pastor was quite clearly trying hard to warm the occasion, but everything else combined to overpower his attempts. The service simply felt cold. It may have been the building. It may have been the stone faces of the choir. It may have been that the manner of leading the order of service seemed to require the congregation to serve the text rather than the text serving their prayer and praise. The service limped to an end. The traveler, who more frequently than she would have liked had been a visitor away from home, wondered again why anybody goes to church. Surely, the perseverance of congregations in such services must be testimony to the power of the Holy Spirit!

A note in the bulletin indicated that the second service was new. The notice described it as "contemporary," and directed newcomers to the fellowship hall. Out of curiosity, and with no other Sunday morning agenda, the visitor decided to investigate. In the fellowship hall, she found rows of folding chairs that had been set up in straight lines, with a center aisle. An electronic keyboard, a drum set, and a row of three standing microphones stood in front and to her left. In the center was a screen with curtains on either side. There was lots of clear glass in the fellowship hall, and the colors of the room were warm. The lighting contributed to the sense of warmth, and the people were chatting in friendly tones among themselves, although no one took particular notice of a visitor. The gathering congregation included lots of children, and many people appeared to be in their thirties or forties, although a number of older people were there.

An usher handed the visitor a bulletin, which outlined a simple order of service. It was not designed primarily as a seeker service, but rather as a worship alternative for church members, first of all, as well as for others who might be attracted by it. The prelude began, in the form of music by the combo. Their playing was of professional quality. The music was upbeat and listenable. The visitor was not a connoisseur of popular music, but it sounded to her more or less like soft rock from the '70s.

A pastor welcomed the people, and a member of the congregation made a series of announcements. A trio of young women made their way to the microphones, and on the screen appeared the words of a song, projected by a computer. The congregation remained seated to sing, probably because if they had stood it would be difficult for some to see the screen. The vocal trio knew their stuff, and along with the combo provided the support necessary for singing. The song was rather long, with lots of repetition, and the tune wasn't distinguished, but people sang with gusto. It didn't seem to matter whether or not all agreed on the melody. Two or three similar pieces followed.

The minister prayed. He called the children forward for a story, then dismissed them. The minister read a short passage from a Bible he held in his hand and, using a music stand for a pulpit, preached the same sermon our visitor had heard at the service in the sanctuary. Another prayer, the Lord's Prayer, more singing, and a benediction followed.

WHAT THE CONTEMPORARY SERVICE WAS LIKE

The basic order of the "contemporary" service was not greatly different from the order of the "traditional" service. The differences between the two seemed to be that in the so-called contemporary service, the congregation never participated verbally except in the singing of a succession of songs, and everything but the singing seemed to have been diminished in size. There was only one reading from Scripture, and no use of scriptural language or allusions except in the songs. The language of the service was colloquial. Prayer was brief and did not reach beyond the immediate time and place. The first-person pronouns used in prayers and songs were almost invariably singular rather than plural—"I" rather than "We," as though the assembly was not the body of Christ, but merely a group of isolated individuals all doing their devotions at the same time. The people remained seated throughout. The word "minimal" came to our visitor's mind. However, the service had a warmer feel because the fellowship hall had a good deal of natural light, the ceiling was lower than in the sanctuary, and people were sitting in closer proximity to one another and to the preaching minister and the musicians. Nevertheless, they had been seated in rows, looking straight ahead, exactly as people in the upstairs sanctuary had sat in the pews.

Visually, the contemporary service was also minimal. There were no Christian symbols, no pulpit, no permanent stand for the Bible. There was no font, nor any reminder that baptisms might occur in this place. There was no Communion table. The visual focal points were the screen and the musicians with their instruments and microphones.

Our visitor went back to her hotel pondering her Sunday morning experiences. How might one perceive the God being worshiped in these two services? She recognized that, as one coming in from outside and only that one time, she probably didn't experience either service in the same way as people who were a part of the continuing congregation. Nevertheless, when she tried to put it into words for a church friend back home, she concluded that at the first service, God had seemed cold, distant, almost historical. At the second service, God had seemed accessible, friendly– but altogether too small. The words of the songs flashed on the screen had spoken of God in majestic terms, but the sense of majesty was absent. Like much of the service, God seemed easy-going, undemanding—minimal.

In many cases, the service with the "contemporary" label can best be understood as a protest and a cry for relief. The unfortunately labeled "traditional" service hasn't been subjected to a serious theological or liturgical critique for many years, if ever. It may be that the pastor, or the director of music, or the congregation itself has established a pattern of resisting any evaluation. The service may simply repeat itself, Sunday after Sunday, with little or no expenditure of time or energy to plan it. The minister plugs in Scripture and sermon title, the musician lists anthem and organ pieces, and one of them chooses three hymns from the hymnal. Not infrequently, if the congregation has been asked to do, say, or sing anything out of their routine, voices among them will object strenuously on behalf of them all. No thought is given to members of the congregation who do not come to worship, nor to newcomers who might wander in. The goal has been simply to play it safe, to give no occasion for criticism by the congregation, and to satisfy those people who are already within the fold.

Some, dissatisfied, leave the congregation and wander off in search of another, without knowing exactly what it is they are looking for. Others, alarmed by the departures of their friends and feeling spiritually undernourished themselves, press the leadership of the congregation for a remedy. The pastor and church officers sense that it would be too disruptive to introduce any change in the established diet of worship, and aren't sure exactly what they would do to change things, anyway. Having heard about "contemporary" services, and knowing that such things exist in their very neighborhood, the solution seems to be to create a new service that will be different from whatever is already in place.

A CRY FOR HELP

So far, so good! However inarticulately, some members of the congregation have tried to put their finger on something lacking. The congregational leadership has decided not to ignore the plea for help. They propose to initiate a new service, not like the old one. But it's at precisely this point that a great deal is at stake. It's not uncommon for those designing the new service to be guided chiefly by their gripes with the established service. The result is a service that is designed as a kind of anti-service. It flows from grievances, real or perceived, against the old.

Is the established service too formal? The new one will be informal. (Not uncommonly, no time is taken to define those terms.) Is the music at eleven o'clock too classical, too elitist? Too closely identified with an older generation? In the new service, the music will be exactly the opposite. Do people feel uncomfortable unless they are wearing their Sunday best? At the new service, people can come as they are. Are Christian symbols puzzling, not visually familiar or easily understood? We'll strip the place of anything that seems exotic so that the worship space resembles the bank, the mall, or the cineplex. Do sacraments seem like hocus-pocus? We'll jettison font and table. Does a sermon by a robed minister seem too structured? We'll ditch the robe and turn the sermon into a talk, and perhaps we'll set the stage for the minister's talk with a staged drama. Do biblical texts clutter the message? We'll talk about relevant matters—dealing with stress at work or in the family, how to recover when love goes sour, making crucial career decisions, parenting a difficult child.

It's absolutely true that one can make a strong case for scrutinizing a church's worship life, and for critiquing it to review where it needs to be changed or strengthened. The culture in which we live is constantly in motion, requiring every aspect of church life to be continually reviewed. This is nothing new. It has always been true, and the church we know is not the same church we knew in 1950 or 1900. However, when reviewing the worship life of the church, one ought to begin at the center rather than at the edges. To proceed on the basis of a catalog of dissatisfactions can easily distort the process, particularly since people in congregations very often do not know how to express their dissatisfactions in a way that points ahead. A recitation of dissatisfactions points backwards. It's an effort to diagnose. The prescription necessary may require of us something more than simply to undo what's usually been done in worship. Rather, it may require us to begin at the beginning—to start with the central things rather than at the edges of the problem. In other words, to start (to use Lathrop's terms) with Bath, Book, and Meal, and attentiveness to the poor.

POSTMODERN

What might worship look like when it takes seriously both the central things and the postmodern era taking shape around us and among us? Postmodern, of course, is a slippery term. More adequate labels for historical epochs are likely to turn up long after those epochs have already jelled, and even after they have passed. For now, however, we'll resort to this word, which doesn't reveal so much about what the new era will be as about what it is not. We no longer live in the modern era. Something new is afoot, and for lack of something better, we'll call it postmodern.

The notion that there is one way, and only one way, to worship springs from the Council of Trent, that post-Reformation Roman Catholic reaction to the Protestant reforms. Before Trent, worship among Catholics was recognizably similar, but not identical from one center to the other. After Trent, there was for the first time a single liturgical text for the Latin Mass. It's not too surprising, then, that even many Protestants harbor an unexamined presumption that if we could only figure out which way is the "right" way to worship, we would all practice that way and that way only. But the fact is, within a common framework, a certain amount of diversity has been the norm from as early as we can trace Christian worship practices. Diversity will, no doubt, continue to be the norm in the postmodern era. No one model for authentic Christian worship will win the day. I offer one example of a possible Lord's Day service not to foreclose other possibilities, but in an attempt to demonstrate a way of being responsive both to the Great Tradition and to contemporary culture.

The setting for such a service might be the sanctuary of a small church in a small town. Many such churches exist. Very likely, the shape of the building itself will reflect the presumptions and values of an earlier era. Our task will be to do a new thing within the constraints imposed by the architecture of another time. That's not easy, because the building speaks with an extraordinarily loud voice. The layout of the sanctuary may make it difficult for people to get up and move around. The three essential focal points—font, pulpit, and table—may all be obscured or miniaturized. Or one of them—usually the pulpit—may dominate the others to the point of overshadowing them. In some churches, the focal point of attention will be a set of organ pipes. There's no question, perhaps, of building a new sanctuary. Nor will the congregation tolerate any suggestion that the interior be gutted in order to re-create the sacred space. So, we will look for ways of making the best of a less than optimal situation.

SUNDAY MORNING

It's Sunday morning. The education hour has finished, and people are beginning to arrive in the sanctuary. The pastor chooses to stand at the door of the church as people enter. She greets each one warmly. Or she goes into the sanctuary, moving from person to person, group to group, saying "Good morning!" and shaking a hand here and there, and, in some cases, receiving a hug. The sanctuary is awash with people greeting one another as they enter. Then, the pastor leaves to prepare for worship.

In her study, she robes in preparation for the service. She has chosen to wear a simple alb, perhaps the color of ripe wheat, or maybe white, with no academic insignia. Unlike an academic gown, her robe is relatively inexpensive and can be easily altered. Perhaps the pastor wears a stole in the color of the liturgical season, and perhaps not. The pastor dons the alb not to call attention to herself, but as a sign that she has a special role to play in the assembly. Others will wear special clothing as well. When the small choir appears, they will be robed. A middle-school student who will read Scripture wears a simple alb. A deacon who will lead the intercessions wears an alb provided for him. In this congregation, worship leadership is usually distributed among several persons. They all wear special dress to add dignity to the occasion.

At the appointed hour, the pastor enters the sanctuary and takes a seat near the Communion table. The noise level subsides somewhat when she rises and stands at the table for a moment. Soon, all eyes notice her presence, and the noise of greetings is hushed. She does not say "Good morning." The minister has taken a new role as a representative officer. It's no longer appropriate to exchange common greetings, because the congregation and its minister are being called to stand together before God. She says, "The grace of the Lord Jesus Christ be with you all." The congregation has been trained to respond, "And also with you." Then, using the simple and direct invitation that has served so many generations, she says, simply, "Let us worship God." As soon as they have exchanged these greetings, the prelude begins. Some continue to enter the sanctuary, and there is still a quiet buzz as each finds a place, but for the most part the congregation has become nearly silent, understanding that the prelude is a part of their worship.

The prelude may be an organ voluntary. After all, there is an organ in this sanctuary. But it may be played by an instrumental ensemble—a group of adults and high school students who have rehearsed together until they can play reasonably well some piece that may or may not be familiar to those gathered. It may be an eclectic group, with a trumpet or two, a trombone, a violin and a viola, a flute and a clarinet. The prelude itself may have a meditative character, or, depending on the occasion, it may have a strong beat and a sense of joyful exuberance. A skillful percussionist, who knows how to support the music rather than dominate it, may participate. Maybe the prelude will include one or more hymns, psalms, or spiritual songs that the congregation will sing later, during the service. On another Sunday, the prelude might be played on an electronic keyboard, or on the piano, or a combo of electric guitars and keyboard, or by the handbell group. Whoever it is, and whatever they play, the pastor has worked with the musicians to understand the various roles that music plays in worship, and to help them understand the flow of the service. She has discussed with them the Scriptures to be read this morning and talked about the people and situations for whom the church will certainly be praying today.

Instead of a prelude, the congregation may begin its worship by singing some gathering music. If there is a choir, they will help to support the singing. If there is no choir, a cantor—a person whose voice can guide the singing—will be there to assist the people's song. The gathering music may begin with a quiet, meditative piece from the Taizé community, or a chant from Iona. The choir or cantor may lead two or three pieces in sequence, moving from a meditative tone toward more lively music that accents joyful praise.

BEFORE GOD AND ONE ANOTHER

When prelude or gathering music finish, the pastor rises and takes a place behind or next to the Communion table. She may begin by stretching out her hands toward the people and calling out, "The Lord be with you." The congregation responds in the same way, with hands outstretched toward her, and the response, "And also with you." There follow words of Scripture, perhaps from one of the readings for the day, or most likely, a portion of the psalm of the day. She may speak those words herself, or, if there is a printed bulletin, she and the congregation may recite them responsively, or one side of the congregation may speak a line while the other side responds with the next line. On some Sundays, the third grade church school class, or the fifth grade, may call the people to worship. They have learned how to say "The Lord be with you/And also with you" with their voices and with their outstretched arms, and they have memorized a short piece of the day's psalm.

The congregation members rise to sing. They may sing from the hymnal, or they may sing a hymn or spiritual song photocopied in the bulletin (with credit to the publisher). In churches with access to superior technology and an appropriate visual space, they may sing from a text projected on an unobtrusive but easily visible screen.[1] They may sing accompanied by organ or by any number of instruments. The point is that the instrument(s) be strong enough to support the singing of a whole congregation. Sometimes, the congregation may sing a cappella—without accompaniment—but only a hymn or spiritual song they already know very well, and usually instrumental accompaniment will help get them started.

When the congregation has finished the opening hymn or song of praise, the members may remain standing if they can see the baptismal font while on their feet. Otherwise, they will be seated while the pastor goes to the baptismal font. Standing at the font, she will call the people to confession with words drawn from Scripture. The people may offer a prayer of confession as they read together in unison from a printed order of service, or they may add a vocal "Amen" to a prayer articulated by the pastor. If printed in the order of service, the prayer will look on the page more like a poem than like a block of dense prose.

Together, the pastor and people create a time of silence. Then they sing. They may sing something like the ancient, "Lord, have mercy upon us. Christ, have mercy upon us. Lord, have mercy upon us." Or they may sing a refrain from a hymn or gospel song, such as the refrain of "There Is a Balm in Gilead," or a verse from "Amazing Grace," such as "Through many dangers, toils and snares we have already come; 'tis grace has brought us safe thus far, and grace will lead us home." Then, the pastor raises a pitcher used to pour water into the font at baptisms, and slowly pours out water into the partially filled font. The pitcher is held high so that it can be seen and so that the sound of the splashing water can be heard. Or the pastor lifts up water from the font in her hands and lets it splash back into the font. She may even take small handfuls and throw the water into the air. (I hope there will be a smile on her face, since this is meant to be playful!) As she pours or splashes or tosses the water into the air, she will declare to the people in scriptural words that God has forgiven them for Jesus' sake. Then, the congregation may sing again, some brief praise to God, our Redeemer. "The peace of the Lord Jesus Christ be with you all," the pastor says. "And also with you," the congregation replies, as each turns to a neighbor to offer some sign of peace. Then, all sit down.

REVERENCE FOR HOLY SCRIPTURE

Cued by instrument(s), choir, or cantor, the congregation sings again. As they sing, a high school student comes from the rear of the sanctuary, walking at a measured pace, carrying in outstretched arms a large pulpit Bible. She or he hands it to the pastor, who carries it to the pulpit and opens it deliberately and reverently. When the people have been seated, the pastor says, "Let us pray," and offers a Prayer for Illumination, asking God to bless the reading, proclaiming, and hearing of the Word by the power of the Holy Spirit, that in these actions the risen Christ may become present to the assembly. The people add their "Amen."

The pastor pauses, smoothes the pages of the large Bible, looks up at the people, and says, "A reading from the prophet Isaiah." Then she reads the passage with great dignity, having read it aloud in her study several times before daring to read it aloud to the congregation. When the Old Testament reading is done, the congregation sings the psalm for the day, or a portion of it. The psalm for the day comments or responds to the first reading in some way. They sing it in a metrical version, perhaps, or it may be that the choir or a cantor will introduce a refrain for the congregation to learn. If the choir or cantor chants the verses of the psalm, they will cue the congregation after each verse or a series of verses, and the congregation will sing the refrain. Singing a psalm, the congregation will add their voices to that great company of Jews and Christians who have sung the psalter from ancient times, and Protestants will join the song of their own forebears who sang Scripture before ever they learned to sing hymns.

A middle-school student, wearing an alb, steps up to the pulpit to read from the Letter to the Romans. In the congregation, two or three people work with the readers. One has been a speech teacher. Another once worked for a radio station, and another has been involved with local theater groups. Each takes turns meeting during the week with the person who will be reading Scripture the subsequent Sunday, and together they discuss the meaning of the text to be read. They discuss which are the most important words, and where the accents should fall within each line. They talk about where the reader might pause most effectively, and about how long the pause should be. Then they practice, with the reader reading the passage aloud. Perhaps they record the reading, so that the reader can hear how he sounds. Today, the young reader reads effectively in a clear, audible voice. Last week, a sixth-grader read, and next week, a woman whose eighty-year-old voice is beautifully mellow.

If the choir, or a children's choir, should sing an anthem, when it's concluded the pastor calls out, "And all the people of God say . . ." and the congregation answers "Amen!" The pastor is giving the people an opportunity to respond appropriately, affirming the choir's offering as their own. This, in contrast to those congregations which mistakenly believe that, in the case of children at least, they must applaud to show their approbation. The pastor has written articles in the newsletter to help people understand that the choirs are not performing for the congregation, but in their music are making an offering to God on behalf of the whole assembly. The "Amen" confirms this way of understanding the choir's contribution and at the same time satisfies the congregation's urge to express their appreciation for this offering made on their behalf.

Preparing to preach, the pastor then steps into the pulpit to read the gospel. (Or, if her text is from the epistle, the reader will have read the gospel and she will read from Romans.) When the preacher says "The Word of the Lord," she raises the pulpit Bible in the air as the people respond, "Thanks be to God."

THE WORD PREACHED

The preacher understands that the pulpit itself, as a piece of ecclesiastical furniture, makes an important symbolic statement, so she reads and preaches from the pulpit. However, in the last congregation she served, the pulpit felt very distant from the congregation. It seemed as though she were preaching across a great gulf. Working with the worship committee, she had suggested that the pulpit be moved, or rebuilt in a more favorable relation to the seated congregation. However, this project had met with stiff resistance, and it seemed better to abandon it. So, reluctantly, she had to weigh two values against each other: the symbolic value of reading and preaching in a place set aside and sanctified for that purpose on the one hand, or nearness to the people on the other. She decided that, for communication's sake, she would choose nearness to the people.

She began to preach from the floor level of the sanctuary, at the head of the center aisle, using a small lectern or a music stand to hold her notes. At times, she even moved away from a fixed position as she preached. However, she did not want to lose the link between Scripture read and the proclamation of the Word, either actually or symbolically. She was committed to preaching from Scripture, and wanted the congregation to see the link between Scripture and sermon as well as discern it in her preaching. It was her decision, then, to read Scripture from the place where she preached. It was important to read not from a small Bible, or from a sheet of paper, even though they would have been more portable. She determined to read from the pulpit Bible, the large Bible from which the other texts had been read. So, before she read her text, she stepped up to the pulpit, received the large Bible from the reader, and carried it to the place from which she would preach her sermon. Usually, the person who had read one of the other texts would walk with her and help her hold the big volume from which she would read. Afterward, the reader would return the large book to the pulpit.

The pastor had a different view of preaching than many of the people in the congregation would have been able to articulate. She knew that she wasn't lecturing on the Bible, or on church doctrine. Although she hoped that people would learn from her sermon, she did not think of the sanctuary as a classroom or of the congregation as pupils. She believed that the act of reading Scripture and preaching from it had a sacramental function. She knew that it had been the experience of the church from early times that Scripture and preaching somehow mediate the presence of the risen Christ, not unlike the ways that baptism and the Lord's Supper mediate Christ's presence. In the case of preaching, the Spirit delivers Christ to the assembly by means of a human voice, personality, and embodied presence.

The pastor has developed a renewed appreciation for the poetic quality of Scripture. She doesn't feel compelled to flatten out every metaphor, or torture every parable into a doctrine. She has learned from various theories of preaching without marrying any one of them. She may use narrative; she may speak personally; she may explain puzzling things in a discursive way. But she respects metaphor, and will often interpret metaphor with another metaphor. To help people grasp a parable, she may speak in parabolic language, offering a contemporary parable or two to offer perspective on the scriptural story. She tries to engage her right brain as well as her preferred left brain. The pastor deeply appreciates the sacramental possibilities of the preached Word, and prepares for it with diligent study and passionate engagement in mind, heart, and soul with the Lord of the text.

RESPONDING TO THE WORD

In this church, the pastor offers an invitation to discipleship after the sermon. It may be as simple as reciting a verse of Scripture or inviting people's commitment (or recommitment) to Jesus Christ. In some places, it may seem good to encourage those who wish to begin a journey of discipleship to come forward and declare their intention, and receive the congregation's prayer and blessing.

The sermon, or invitation, might be followed by a hymn and a creed of the church. When the congregation affirms its faith using a creed, it's not a piece of prose they had never seen before—certainly not composed by the pastor—but something that belongs to the whole ecumenical church. Or they might sing something like "We All Believe in One True God" or "I Believe in God Almighty," sung versions of the Apostles' Creed.[2] It may be that contemporary pieces could serve a similar purpose. Creeds like the Apostles' and the Nicene are poetic in their format. The poetic form communicates in a subtle way that this is not meant to be a scientific formula but an affirmation of biblical faith in all its multivalent richness. In Calvin's Geneva, the congregation sang the creed, which served even more effectively to make clear that it's not meant as a theological argument but as a kind of doxology, an act of praise anchored in Scripture and in the faith of the church. When the congregation sings a creed, somehow there's less tendency to argue with it. Its doxological nature is apparent, even if people have never heard the word "doxological."

Every congregation has people who don't understand the creed, or who think they understand it well enough to disagree with this part of it or some other part. Its use, nevertheless, offers us an opportunity to grow into the mature faith it represents. If at some point it irritates, the irritation may stimulate the kind of questioning and reflection that leads to growth.

Perhaps once a year, maybe twice, there is opportunity in this service for members of the congregation to reaffirm the covenant made in their baptism. The gospel reading for the day may have been one of the stories of Jesus' baptism by John, and the sermon may have been drawn from that text. The pastor may pour water into the font, and ask the congregation to renounce evil and to profess their faith, just as at baptism. The Apostles' Creed may be used here, instead of in response to the sermon, and it may take an interrogatory form ("Do you believe in God? . . . in Jesus Christ? . . . in the Holy Spirit?"), since that creed is so closely linked to the sacrament of baptism. Then, the pastor may invite members of the congregation to come forward, if they wish, to receive the laying on of hands and, perhaps, anointing with oil. As each comes to stand before a minister or other officer of the church, he says his first name aloud, and the minister or elder places a hand on his head and says,

> Defend, O Lord, your servant [name]
> with your heavenly grace, that [he/she] may continue
>   yours forever,
> and daily increase in your Holy Spirit more
>   and more, until [he/she]
> comes to your everlasting kingdom.[3]

The congregant may have heard these words somewhere before— in the baptismal service, or when members of the confirmation class made their first public profession of faith. But this time, the words are for that individual and, though not the first time, the touch of the hand, the saying of the name, the fragrance of the oil, remind each one that he or she is a precious child of God. The God who claimed each in their baptism still claims them, and once again, they pledge themselves to the One who knows them by name.

Or an actual baptism may occur at this point in the service—or, in this congregation, a great many baptisms, since they are grouped together so that the baptismal service can be celebrated in great style from beginning to end of the service rather than simply being sand-wiched in as a sort of aside. This congregation loves to baptize at Easter, early in the new year (the Sunday called the Baptism of the Lord), and at Pentecost. All who bring children for baptism, or who come to be baptized themselves, have met as a group with the pastor and lay leaders, who have introduced them both to the rite itself, to its significance, and to the mutual obligations undertaken by congre-gation, parents, and, in some cases, sponsors.

Today, however, it's a moment for commissioning a group of church school teachers, with solemn pledges of support from the con-gregation and with prayers and blessings. Next Sunday, it will be the moment when the congregation commissions a work crew who will be flying to Central America to participate in a rebuilding project in a community still recovering from earthquake and flood.

PRAYER

It's approaching time for the Prayers of the People. The pastor has cho-sen this place for announcements. Most announcements are available in print, and need no more than a brief reference. The pastor's commitment is to keep the announcements simple and short. She has chosen this point in the service because she wants to mention the names of persons in the congregation who are in special need of the church's prayers. They are sick, or have suffered the loss of a loved one. She mentions them now, just before the congregation will be called to prayers of intercession. She tells the people that Mary Adams is in Good Samaritan Hospital. Hector Gomez has moved to a nursing home. James Chang is ill at home. Margaret Smith has died; we will hold a service for her at the church on Monday.

When the current pastor first arrived, she had wanted to contribute toward the invigoration of the congregation's prayer life. In order not to neglect anyone who carried some concern or burden, she had designated this time in the service one for hearing people's joys and concerns. She invited the congregation to state joys and concerns out loud, but she found that most people were reluctant to do that, while the same few people tended to speak up every Sunday. The pastor decided to take a different tack. Each Sunday's bulletin contained a slip of paper on which people could write prayer requests. (In the congregation she had served last, they had not used a printed bulletin, so similar slips had been placed at the doors or in the pews.) The person offering the Prayers of the People walked among the congregation, collecting the slips of paper as they were passed to him. The pastor was struck by the deep concern members of the congregation felt for family, friends, neighbors, and work colleagues who were experiencing illnesses or grief. She was moved by those who felt the need to express their gratitude for some person or circumstance, and she could sense the congregation's empathy for those facing difficult decisions.

The pastor herself did not usually offer the Prayers of the People. Instead, the moderator of the board of deacons, or some other deacon she might designate, ordinarily led these prayers. It was, after all, the board of deacons who were responsible for visiting the sick and the grieving. It was the deacons who occasionally came to the rescue when a family in the congregation fell into crisis due to unemployment of the key wage earner. It was the board of deacons who had been studying the lack of elder housing in the community, and who had involved the congregation in hosting homeless people periodically, in rotation with other churches. And so, it seemed logical that when the congregation began to pray for the world and for themselves, a deacon might be a powerful symbol of the ways the congregation's active ministry and its ministry of prayer go together.

The pastor spends time with the deacons, assisting them in this ministry of leading the people's prayers, and particularly with the moderator who ordinarily prays in the assembly on Sunday morning. The deacons have learned how to pray for the whole church, of every confession and on every continent, and for those who minister in it. They have learned to pray for all the nations, and for our own nation, and for those in authority. They pray for peace and justice in the world, for the proper use of the earth and its resources. They pray for their own community, and particularly the poor and the oppressed. When natural disasters occur, or when people hear distressing national or international news, these became occasions for prayer. A major corporation has threatened to close a local factory, affecting 650 employees, and this concern has found its way into the church's prayers. The deacon prays for the sick and the shut-in and the grieving by first name—for Mary, for Hector, for James, for the grieving family of your servant Margaret. And then, of course, the deacon reads the slips of paper with the many concerns and thanksgivings the congregation has asked to include in the prayers.

They pray standing up, with people on each side of the aisle facing toward the aisle and therefore toward one another. In this way, they try to create a stronger sense of a gathered community, in spite of the constraints imposed by the traditional sanctuary with its fixed pews. The deacon prays from the middle of the aisle, in the midst of the people. After a few petitions, the deacon says, "In your mercy, Lord," and the congregation answers, "Hear our prayer." Or, when the deacon says, "In your mercy, Lord," someone sounds a note, and all sing. Sometimes it's something like "Jesus, remember me, when you come into your kingdom." Sometimes it's something like "Someone's praying, Lord, kum ba yah! Someone's praying, Lord, kum ba yah! Someone's praying, Lord, kum ba yah! O Lord, kum ba yah!" or "Spirit of the living God, fall afresh on us; Spirit of the living God, fall afresh on us."

As the people pray, led by the deacon, some of them have one or both hands opened, palms upward, as though anticipating something that will fill them, or perhaps as a symbolic offering of themselves. A few have folded their hands in the familiar prayer posture they learned as children. These are members of a mainline congregation, so it would be unusual to see someone raising a hand in the air, although sometimes the deacon has invited people to raise both hands in the air as they pray the Lord's Prayer. In this way, they imitate the posture of Jewish prayer in the first century, and at the same time create a rather quiet and unthreatening form of liturgical dance. The pastor harbors a hope that the congregation might learn to be a little looser, a bit more bodily *present*, feeling free to accompany acts of worship with some physical signs of their participation. She is neither a Pentecostal nor charismatic, but she appreciates that the inner self may follow where the body leads.

WHERE THE BODY LEADS

The pastor had read about a study done in a university town. The researchers had enlisted a group of university students, and told them that they were going to be testing a new brand of headset. The purpose, they explained, was to see how the headsets functioned when the person wearing them was in motion. They divided the students into three groups. All three groups heard a recording that featured music by Linda Ronstadt, followed by a radio editorial urging that tuition at the local university be raised from the current $587 to $750. The researchers directed one group of students to shake their heads back and forth as they listened. They told the second group to nod their heads vigorously up and down as they listened. They gave the third group no instructions. At the conclusion, the researchers asked each student to answer a brief questionnaire. The last question asked what the students thought would be an appropriate dollar amount per year for tuition at their university. The group that had been instructed to shake their heads back and forth were vigorous in their disapproval of the radio editorial. They thought tuition should be *lowered* to $467. The students who had been instructed to nod their heads up and down thought that tuition should be *raised* to $646. The control group thought tuition should remain about what it was.[4]

When the pastor read about this study, it drew her attention to the fact that little things we do—even such apparently trivial things as physical movements—can influence the way we perceive things and feel about them. This confirmed her own experience as her practices in leading worship had evolved from standing before the people with a book or paper in hand to the use of posture and movement that represented in body language the significance of the words she was using.

With that in mind, she has reflected on ways that she could encourage her congregation to learn simple movements and gestures appropriate to prayer and praise that she believes will contribute to a re-forming of their inner lives.

When the deacon concludes the Prayers of the People, he invites the people to create a time of silence. Perhaps he will ask them to sit. The pastor knows that the conventional wisdom is that younger generations don't like "dead time," and therefore can't be expected to tolerate silence. But she has learned to distinguish between "dead time," which is marked by an absence of sound, and silence kept, which is a positive creation of the assembly. Some bow their heads and close their eyes. Others simply shut their eyes. Others fix their gaze on a cross, or candles, or the ceiling. No one exhorts the congregation to "use" the silence, as though it were a piece of work to be done. If their minds wander, they are encouraged simply to let them wander. It's all offered to God. The people have learned to cherish the silence. Adolescents take it seriously, and even children respect it. When younger children fuss, the congregation is learning not to get distressed.

THE FEAST

The prayers concluded, the deacon uses words from Scripture to invite people to make their offerings. The offering is a bridge between the service of the Word and the service of the table. In the early church, people would bring from their homes bread and wine from their own supplies. They would leave these gifts on a table near the entrance to the place of assembly. Then, during the service, the deacons would take from among them bread and wine enough to use for the Lord's Supper, leaving the rest to be distributed to the poor following the service. When the Scriptures had been read, the Word proclaimed, and those not yet initiated had been dismissed, officers would process to the holy table with the bread and wine to be used in the sacramental celebration.

The offering in our own church, then, is not just a device to try to shake money out of folks while they are feeling spiritually minded. It grows out of that early practice. In this service, as the people's tithes and offerings of money are brought forward, two or three members of the congregation also accompany them, bearing a loaf of bread and a pitcher, which they offer to the minister presiding at the table. While the pastor places the offering plates on another table nearby to receive them, she places the bread and the pitcher on the Communion table, to be used in the Lord's Supper.

The pastor offers, in scriptural words, an invitation to all the baptized to accept the hospitality of the Lord's Table, which itself is a reaffirmation of the covenant made at their baptism. Then the congregation sits, as they would in their own kitchens or dining rooms, and they sing a hymn, a psalm, or a spiritual song related to the sacrament. The presiding minister then issues an invitation to children and young people to come forward and join her, standing as close to her and to the holy table as possible. They bring with them a text of the Great Prayer of Thanksgiving, which the minister will pray at the table. Some of them are too young to read, but they have become familiar with their role because in this congregation they celebrate the Lord's Supper every Sunday.

The pastor understands that the Great Prayer of Thanksgiving at the Lord's Table essentially belongs to the church. Her role is to articulate the church's prayer. It's the church's celebration, and the congregation are the celebrants. She is the presider. The celebrants who are able stand for this prayer. Because it has a long, long history, the pastor chooses to permit herself to be tutored by the Great Church, which has prayed in thanksgiving over the loaf and cup since New Testament times. The congregation knows their part of the opening dialogue: "The Lord be with you!" the pastor cries. "And also with you," the congregation answers. The children, gathered around her, extend a hand toward her as they respond. "Lift up your hearts!" she exhorts, and as she does, she slowly lifts her hands high into the air, palms upward. "We lift them to the Lord," the people answer. "Let us give thanks to the Lord our God," she says, shaping her hands into a prayer-like posture. All reply, "It is right to give our thanks and praise."

The children and youth know that this is their cue to ask, "Why do we give thanks and praise before this table?" and the congregation and the presiding minister answer together, "We give thanks for God's work of creation, liberation, and salvation." Throughout the prayer, the children will ask a series of questions, to which the presiding minister will respond, very much like the ritual of the Passover Seder, when the youngest child asks, "Why is this night different from all other nights?" and the person presiding offers the answer that has been given for generations at similar meals. The pastor then continues the Great Prayer of Thanksgiving. She extends her hands, palms open as a way of gathering and blessing both the congregation and the bread and wine. Members of the congregation may also extend a hand toward the holy table.

She may have the text of the Great Thanksgiving on a small stand in front of her on the Communion table, or she may frame the prayer in her own words, carefully thought through before her arrival at the church on Sunday morning. In any case, she knows that, although the precise words may vary, a pattern has shaped this prayer since early generations. The form is Trinitarian, thanking and praising God for the creation, and for God's work in covenant history and through the prophets, and for God's watchful care in spite of human failure. Thanking and praising God for God's work of redemption in Jesus Christ, remembering his birth, life, ministry, his death and resurrection and ascension, his continual intercession for us and looking for his coming again. And calling on the Holy Spirit to lift us all into Christ's presence, to nourish us with the body and blood of Christ, to make us one with Christ and all God's people, and to keep us faithful as Christ's body on earth.

HOLY! HOLY! HOLY!

The threefold form is simple, and she doesn't forget it even when she prays without looking at a text. She also is mindful to give the proper verbal cues so that the congregation and the children and young people know where to join their voices, for this prayer is one in which there is active participation. After thanking and praising the first person of the Trinity, she calls on everyone present to join in the worship of the heavenly court, adding our voices to their "unending praise." The instrument(s) give the signal, and the congregation sings

> Holy, holy, holy Lord, God of power and might,
> Heaven and earth are full of your glory,
> Hosanna in the highest. Blessed is he who comes
>   in the name of the Lord.
> Hosanna in the highest, hosanna in the highest.

They sing in full voice, because they know this song. They know it as well as many congregations know the Doxology or the Gloria Patri. When she gives the verbal cue, the children and youth ask, "Why do we eat bread at this table?" and she responds with the first half of the

Words of Institution from 1 Corinthians 11: "On the night before he died, Jesus took bread . . ." Then they ask, "Why do we drink from the cup at this table?" and she finishes the Scriptural quote with the words that refer to the cup of the new covenant. Then they ask, "What do we remember at this table?" and she continues the prayer, "We remember God's gracious love for us, Christ's death and resurrection for us, and the Spirit's tender care for us." Then she calls out, "Let us proclaim the mystery of faith." The whole congregation bursts into song,

> Dying, you destroyed our death,
> rising, you restored our life.
> Lord Jesus, come in glory!

She prays for the Spirit's action in this celebration, and ends the prayer with an ascription of praise to the Holy Trinity to which all say "Amen!" and then all pray the Lord's Prayer.

The children and youth return to their places with their parents or friends. Then, the whole congregation comes forward and forms something like a crowded circle around the Communion table. (This congregation would not hear of removing the pews and replacing them with durable but flexible seating, but they did consent to permit the removal of two pews in order to provide room to gather at the table.) As they come forward and throughout the Communion they sing, with occasional pauses for silence. They don't sing mournful tunes, unless you count the rather meditative pieces for Ash Wednesday or Maundy Thursday. They sing joyful songs, appropriate to a celebration and a welcoming of the risen Lord. They may sing a cappella, led by someone with the skills to lead, or they may sing accompanied by one or more instruments.

Sometimes servers move among the people, breaking pieces off the two halves of the loaf and placing them in the palms of the people, followed by the cup. The communicants may dip the bread into the cup. However, this congregation has purchased chalices with a pouring lip, so it's possible for the servers or ministers to pour from it into smaller cups, which the people are given as they come to the table. At other times, the baskets containing the two halves of the broken loaf are simply passed among the people, who serve themselves and each other. Trays of individual cups follow, passed from hand to hand. In a congregation where the pastor had served on the staff, the size of the congregation was large enough that it worked better when people came forward in two lines, receiving first the bread, then the cup, from servers stationed at the front of the church. In any case, there are places to return empty cups when individual cups have been used.

LED FORTH IN PEACE

All remain at or near the holy table for the remainder of the service. Some move into the chancel, sharing it with the members of the choir. Others stand around or alongside the table, or, when there are many people, a few feet into the aisles. There are children; elderly people; teenagers; one family's autistic son; Freda's mother, who suffers from some sort of senile dementia—all close to one another. Even on Sundays when few are present, they feel the power of the gathering when they collect together in close proximity to the table and to one another. When everyone has been served, the presiding minister offers a prayer of thanksgiving for the sacrament. It may be that this will be the place for extending the peace of Christ, rather than after the Prayer of Confession. In that case, everyone shakes a hand, offers an embrace or a kiss on the cheek.

Cued once again to sing, the congregation breaks out in song. They need neither hymnal nor printed text, because they sing it every Sunday. It's a paraphrase of words from Isaiah 55:12. It goes,

> For you shall go out in joy,
>   and be led back in peace;
> the mountains and the hills before you
>   shall burst into song,
>   and all the trees of the field shall clap,
>   their hands.

As they sing, they all raise their hands and clap. Then they sing it again. Even the most reserved can be seen to be smiling, and the children are filled with delight. The pastor raises her hands toward them, and turning as she speaks, charges them to go out into the world in peace; and then offers a blessing. They linger, departing, it seems, with reluctance.

BROADENING MUSICAL HORIZONS

The music used in this service is eclectic. The pastor works closely with the musician, who teaches in the public schools. They instruct each other, and each profits by the knowledge of the other. Both have attended music and worship conferences sponsored by their denomination. They have found their own hymnal to be a treasury of resources with which it was worthwhile to become acquainted. But they have searched in other places as well.

The congregation has learned to appreciate music originating in the hymnals of other denominations, including the Roman Catholic Church. They have been responsive to African American music, and have enjoyed learning hymns from other parts of the world— particularly some of the rhythmic hymns from Latin America. The musician and pastor have sifted through collections of so-called "praise songs," or "Scripture choruses," and have found some pieces to use in worship from those sources.

Pastor and musician look at each piece of music with interest in its text, the theology represented in its text, and the integrity of its music. They like to use pieces that the congregation can learn to sing without too much struggle, but they are suspicious of music that sounds like a TV commercial or elevator music or that evokes associations with secular culture strong enough to drown out the religious texts. It needs to stand up under repetition—be "simple enough to be sung relatively well on first hearing and . . . nevertheless substantial enough to continue to inspire the sung prayer."[5]

Musician and pastor look at each piece of music to consider how it might function in the service and how it will relate to other music in the same service. It takes time, but they have decided that good worship can't be planned quickly or offhandedly. Amazingly, the congregation has expanded its musical repertoire considerably, even though a few still complain that they don't get to sing often enough something they loved when they were children. And yet, the pastor and musician have discovered that some of the old nineteenth-century gospel songs have quite a different sound and feel when the meters are altered a bit or when a different instrument is used to accompany them. This congregation has retrieved some music that others had long ago thrown away, just as mainliners rediscovered "Amazing Grace" in the 1960s after decades of ignoring it.

History shows that the greater percentage of music produced in any generation will be forgotten in another generation or two. How much of the music of the Reformation era has endured into the twenty-first century? Ten percent? Twenty? There has been an enormous proliferation of music written for worship over the past fifty years. Some of it will endure. Ten percent? Twenty? Most will soon be forgotten. The pastor-musician team tries to choose new pieces most likely to be durable, but the process is one of trial and error. They have agreed, however, in the course of their discussions, that their goal is to enable the people's song rather than to produce song of performance quality.

CHANGE FOR HOSPITALITY'S SAKE

This congregation has experienced a good deal of change in a short time. The members' capacity to embrace change is itself rather a new thing. For years, they resisted their pastors whenever the pastors tried to initiate change. This was particularly true when it came to worship and to the music used in worship. The congregation is still conservative. Members like their sanctuary as it is. But during the last pastoral vacancy, a consultant appointed by the denomination had led them in a self-study that articulated what many had, at long last, begun to sense. They were losing their own children. Not all their adult children had moved away. Those who remained in town did not frequently remain with the church of their childhood. Faced with the fact that their congregation was fading, the people might have resisted change to the bitter end, but in this case they did not. Realizing that there was a great deal at stake here, a consensus emerged to seek leadership who could help them renew their congregational life. When the new pastor arrived, they gave her the benefit of the doubt. To their credit, they resolved to try as hard as they could to put their personal preferences a bit off to the side—not to discard them, mind you, but to make some sacrifices that might make a positive contribution to the future of the congregation.

Changes in their worship have been significant. The pastor has introduced most of them slowly, incrementally, and often introduced them the first time in smaller groups: the women's group, the men's group, Bible study groups, the Wednesday evening fellowship. The pastor knows that, as important as the church's worship is, there's more to the renewal of congregational life than merely changing worship practices. So, many other initiatives are under way. To the astonishment of the denominational authorities, worship attendance has been growing, and many who at first resisted change have forgotten that they had.

The older members of the congregation made what at first felt like a sacrifice. As younger people have become part of the congregation, they have appreciated what they experience as the hospitality of the longer-term members. A large, independent congregation is located a few miles away, toward the suburbs of the nearby city, and some younger people from the community drive there for worship. But the newer members here appreciate being part of a multigenerational congregation. If not everything seems designed specifically for their generation, they accept it as a worthy trade-off. Old members and new members have each made room for the other, and something true and good has grown up here.

Afterword

Neither Contemporary
nor Traditional

The thesis of this book is that neither of the worship phenomena popularly described as contemporary and traditional will be the wave of the future. Since neither of these terms is precise, I will try to describe what I think these two terms mean in conventional usage. So-called traditional worship is the baseline, since so-called contemporary worship is a reaction to it.

In most writing and conversation about these two styles of worship, the terms are not defined. Nevertheless, those who use the term *traditional* to describe worship seem to make certain presumptions about it. Traditional worship is the kind that people in mainline churches were most likely to be accustomed to in the 1950s. It is most often a service of the Word, in which the sermon is the prominent feature. Very often, the sermon is understood in terms of teaching, or providing spiritual inspiration, or forming opinion on social or personal issues. It may be fair to say that, in many cases, it moralizes rather than theologizes. There may be an emphasis on being sure the congregation understands everything taking place, so that even sacraments suffer from a certain measure of didacticism.

Frequently, the traditional service involves the congregation in a good deal of unison or responsive reading from a printed order of service. Sometimes it seems as though the point is to get through all the words, and all the words are of equal weight. In other words, the printed text dominates the liturgy rather than serving it.

There is no doubt that in the postmodern era we suffer from a crisis of confidence in words. We have been buried in words, flooded with words, assaulted with words. The telephone rings during dinner, and if we are so foolish as to answer it, we encounter someone who wants to persuade us that we are among the fortunate few chosen to be offered a bargain on new windows, or a time-share at the beach, or even a cemetery lot. Commercials make extravagant promises that are scarcely distinguishable from outright lies. People running for office stake out a platform that appears to take our interests very seriously indeed, but about which we have grown skeptical, if not cynical. Bumper stickers and vanity plates amuse us, scold us, scandalize us, and lecture us as we drive to work. And oh, so very many seem to find it easy to speak with supreme confidence about God's will and God's ways, as though they knew the landscape of God's mind better than their own backyards.

God's name is linked with all sorts of hostilities. God hates homosexuals, single parents, Jews, liberals, and taxes, according to those self-selected to report such antagonisms to the rest of us. In a time when words are cheap and easily ignored, worship that relies so very exclusively on words will be in trouble.

THE TONE OF THE TRADITIONAL SERVICE

The tone of the traditional service is cool, with an emphasis on emotional restraint and propriety, although in some cases the presiding minister tries very hard to inject a sense of warmth and informality, which may provoke a feeling of incongruity. In the traditional service, the congregation is not likely to move out of the pews, unless the service is over.

The Lord's Supper may be celebrated on a monthly basis, with the greater emphasis on the cross than on the resurrection. The tone will be sober and reflective rather than celebrative.

The traditional service is likely to include an organ and a choir. The congregation will sing from a hymnal, usually hymns chosen from a limited repertoire, most of which were familiar to congregations before 1970.

Children may be called forward for a children's sermon. The great likelihood is that they will be dismissed after the first few minutes of the service either for an education period or for child care.

Of course, many variations on this theme exist. And some services described as traditional, for want of a better term, do not fit this profile at all. There is still a constituency for the so-called traditional service described above. It may be done very well. Many find its familiarity comforting. When there is strong leadership, it can be attractive. It is, however, clearly shaped by the modern era and by modern sensibilities, which puts it at risk as the modern gives way to the postmodern.

THE CONTEMPORARY SERVICE

If there were no traditional service, there could be no contemporary service. The contemporary service bounces off the traditional. It is, in fact, a kind of anti-service. It has been shaped, most often, by dissatisfaction. What makes it contemporary? The term *contemporary* seems to be simply a means of distinguishing it from what has gone before. It is contemporary in that it's an attempt to address the present-day alienation from the church of those adults who belong to the so-called baby boom generation. It gropes toward something new, more experiential and relational than didactic, but it is more similar to traditional worship than different from it.

Contemporary worship is no more alike in every place than is traditional worship. However, quite typically it has a populist feel to it. The aim is to simulate a kind of '60s egalitarianism, symbolized by casual dress of the congregation and its ministers alike. No matter how much choreography or technical preparation is required, the service is meant to look spontaneous and impromptu.

Contemporary worship is suspicious of any suggestion that past generations should have a voice in the way things are done in today's church. There is a sense that current thinking, tastes, and experience trump anything from the past. Just as machines and technology have become better and better, making all their predecessors obsolete, it seems that we have reached a moment in history in which human beings are morally, intellectually, and spiritually superior to whatever has gone before.

If the past is not relevant, then even Scripture may need to be minimized. One typical result is a colloquial style that banishes liturgical language—that language which is saturated in Scripture and scriptural allusions. Whatever theoretical priority may be given to Scripture, in practice the contemporary worship assembly may be exposed to very little of it.

Contemporary worshipers may value symbols, but usually only the symbols they have created themselves. Symbols inherited from other times and places seem obscure, if not primitive. They have little place in contemporary worship.

Often the single most distinctive characteristic of contemporary worship is its music. Worshipers prefer music that has a familiar sound and beat. Music in conventional meters and harmonies stirs associations with the dreaded word "classical," and seems stuffy, pretentious, and elitist to many baby boomers. In the contemporary service, music for worship must resemble popular music, and make use of instruments familiar from popular culture. It's not uncommon for music in contemporary worship to resemble the music popular two or three decades ago.

MARRYING THE SPIRIT OF THE AGE

The church owes a debt of thanks to the baby boomers for drawing attention to the fact that the modern era is fading and a postmodern era is dawning. The boomers have stimulated reflection and analysis that the church needs to do in these crucial times. At the same time, whenever the church has reinvented its worship simply to address the baby boomers and their generational crises, it has wagered everything on short-run trends, and set itself up for obsolescence in the near future. Like traditional worship, contemporary worship is shaped by the presumptions and sensibilities of the modern era, which is even now passing away. Not only is contemporary worship hopelessly wedded to a single generation—the boomers—but in some ways it reflects modern values even more than traditional worship does. More than a typical 1950s-oriented service of the Word, the so-called contemporary service minimizes the sacraments and silences the voices of any generation but one. It is more wedded to a culture—that of the 1970s, '80s, and '90s—than so-called traditional worship is wedded to the '40s and '50s.

The greater danger is that the crises of the baby boomers have caused many churches to believe that if they want to survive, they will need to tailor worship differently for each successive generation. Not only are mainline Protestant churches notoriously segregated by race and socioeconomic class, but they are in danger of becoming segregated by generation. This not only obscures more than ever the inclusiveness of God's new creation, but it impoverishes the life of congregations. Worship that includes representatives of several generations, from the aged to the very young, is stronger rather than weaker.

However, although traditional worship is probably more inclusive than most contemporary worship, it also has a tendency to segregate by generation. It segregates by generation when it limits its musical vocabulary to one genre, and particularly when it is not hospitable to the presence of children. Christian educators and others concerned about children have insisted for decades that children cannot learn to worship without being a part of the worshiping community. Being segregated from their early years contributes to incapacitating people for worship when they grow older. When the form and content of worship include children only on adult terms, children become unofficially excommunicated.

BEGINNING AT THE CENTER
RATHER THAN THE EDGES

The task before congregations in an emerging postmodern era is not an easy one. The church that is planning for the long run rather than the short run will look beyond feeling forced to choose between apparent polar opposites, defined as traditional or contemporary. Those models are in fact alternatives only within a narrow range.

The congregation that is inclined to look beyond the modern era will begin at the center rather than at the edges. They will take Word and sacrament with equal seriousness, each essential to the health of the other. They will plan for a worshiping congregation that expects the presence of children and intentionally includes them. They will plan for a congregation that, at least in anticipation, looks toward the possibility of including people who represent the increasingly diverse ethnic mix of twenty-first-century North America.

Such a congregation will not categorically rule out the cultural arti-facts of any generation. In such a church, it will be possible to hear the sound of the organ, but not impossible to hear the sounds of per-cussion instruments as well. Some of the music will sound like the nineteenth century, or the sixteenth, or the second, and some will sound like the late twentieth century or the early twenty-first. Some will make the most sophisticated musicians proud, and other music will gladden the hearts of the same musicians because they understand that the music of worship is first and foremost not for performance, but for enabling the people's song.

Most of all, the church that begins its review and reform of wor-ship at the center will devote equal attention to the practice of weekly Eucharist alongside passionate preaching. Christian initiation will be undertaken with great seriousness, and with involvement of many members of the congregation in leading inquirers and new Christians ever deeper into the faith and life of the church. Baptism will be made large, far more than routine. As churches rediscover the power of rite, preaching may also become more vivid, less abstract. Will those churches draw huge crowds? The better question is, will those churches be equally attentive to the deep things of the gospel, handed on in the great tradition, and to the new possibilities of contemporary culture?

Notes

Introduction

1. Donald E. Miller, *Reinventing American Protestantism: Christianity in the New Millennium* (Berkeley, Calif.: University of California Press, 1997), 19.

Chapter 1: The So-Called "Worship Wars"

1. Quoted in an essay by Mark Searle, "Looking to the Future," in *The Changing Face of Jewish and Christian Worship in North America*, ed. Paul F. Bradshaw and Lawrence A. Hoffman (Notre Dame, Ind.: University of Notre Dame Press, 1991), 233.
2. H. Richard Niebuhr, *Christ and Culture* (New York: Harper & Brothers, 1956).
3. Robert E. Webber, ed., *The Renewal of Sunday Worship* (Nashville: Star Song, 1993), 124.

Chapter 2: What Folks Are Looking For

1. Richard F. Ward, "Dreaming of New Forms and Utterances: Seeds for Ritual Reformation in a TV Culture," *Reformed Liturgy & Music*, vol. 30, no. 2 (1996): 54.
2. Stanley Hauerwas, quoted in "Are Evangelicals Searching for a More Fragrant Soap?" *Context,* ed. Martin Marty, vol. 31, no. 8 (April 15, 1999): 3.
3. Stephen Mathonnet-Vander Well, quoted in *Context,* ed. Martin Marty, vol. 32, no. 18 (October 15, 2000): 5.
4. Leander Keck, *The Church Confident* (Nashville: Abingdon Press, 1993).
5. Lesslie Newbigin, *The Gospel in a Pluralist Society* (Grand Rapids: Wm. B. Eerdmans Publishing Co., 1989), 151.
6. From the hymn "Love Divine, All Loves Excelling," in *The Presbyterian Hymnal* (Louisville, Ky.: Westminster/John Knox Press, 1990), 376 verse 4: *"Finish, then, Thy new creation; Pure and spotless*

let us be; Let us see Thy great salvation Perfectly restored in Thee; Changed from glory into glory, Till in heaven we take our place, Till we cast our crowns before Thee, Lost in wonder, love, and praise."

7. Ben Patterson, *Serving God: The Grand Essentials of Work & Worship* (Downers Grove, Ill.: InterVarsity Press, 1994), 116–17.

8. J. Randall Nichols, "Worship as Anti-Structure: The Contribution of Victor Turner," *Theology Today* (January 1985): 401.

Chapter 3: Is There Such a Thing as "Traditional Worship"?

1. When I use the terms "deep tradition" or "Great Tradition," I use them both to refer to the long history of worship in the ecumenical church, both East and West, since ancient times. While this tradition is not uniform, it testifies in various ways in different times and places to the great esteem in which the church has held Baptism, Scripture and Preaching, the Lord's Supper, prayer and song throughout the generations. In times of renewal, those with a reforming mission have appealed to the practices and theological insights of other eras or other parts of the church in order to provide a lens through which to examine conventional worship practices and assess strengths and weaknesses in them.

2. E. Glenn Hinson, "Dear Saint Benedict: A Letter of Appreciation for What Your Children Have Meant to Me," *Lexington Theological Quarterly*, vol. 35, no. 1 (spring 2000): 5.

3. Gordon Lathrop, *Holy Things: A Liturgical Theology* (Minneapolis: Fortress, 1993), and Gordon Lathrop, *Holy People: A Liturgical Ecclesiology* (Minneapolis: Fortress Press, 1999).

4. Carlos M. N. Eire, *War Against the Idols: The Reformation of Worship from Erasmus to Calvin* (Cambridge: Cambridge University Press, 1986).

5. Marianne Meye Thompson, "Reflections on Worship in the Gospel of John," *The Princeton Seminary Bulletin*, vol. 19, no. 3, New Series (1998): 268–69.

6. Stephen Mathonnet-Vanderwell, "Reformed Musing on a Post-Christian Culture," in *Perspectives, A Journal of Reformed Thought*, March 2000.

7. Ibid., 6.

8. Ibid., 9.

9. Lesslie Newbigin, *The Gospel in a Pluralist Society* (Grand Rapids: Wm. B. Eerdmans Publishing Co., 1989), 8.

10. Quoted in an essay by Mark Searle, "Looking to the Future," in *The Changing Face of Jewish and Christian Worship in North America,* ed. Paul F. Bradshaw and Lawrence A. Hoffman (Notre Dame, Ind.: University of Notre Dame Press, 1991), 223.

11. Ibid.

12. Ibid, 227.

Chapter 4: Is There Such a Thing as "Contemporary Worship"?

1. Rodger Nishioka, "Finding the 'Lost' Generation," *Reformed Liturgy & Music*, vol. 32, no. 1 (1998): 7.
2. Marva Dawn, *Reaching Out Without Dumbing Down: A Theology of Worship for the Turn-of-the-Century Culture* (Grand Rapids: Wm. B. Eerdmans Publishing Co., 1995).
3. Rob Marus and Marshall Allen, "The New Liturgicals," *Religious Herald: Virginia Baptists' Weekly* (October 7, 1999): 1.
4. J. Randall Nichols, "Worship as Anti-Structure: The Contribution of Victor Turner," *Theology Today* (January 1985): 401.
5. Lester Ruth, "Lex Agendi, Lex Orandi: Toward an Understanding of Seeker Services as a New Kind of Liturgy," *Worship* (September 1996): 386–405.
6. G. A. Pritchard, *Willow Creek Seeker Services: Evaluating a New Way of Doing Church* (Grand Rapids: Baker Books, 1996), 268.
7. Ibid., 269.
8. Suggested by John Witvliet of the Calvin Institute of Christian Worship.
9. Frank Burch Brown, *Good Taste, Bad Taste, & Christian Taste: Aesthetics in Religious Life* (New York: Oxford University Press, 2000), 195.
10. Ibid., 195–96.
11. John D. Witvliet, "The Blessing and Bane of the North American Megachurch: Implications for Twenty-First Century Congregational Song," *The Hymn*, vol. 50, no. 1 (January, 1999): 7.

Chapter 5: The Ecology of Word and Sacrament

1. Howard G. Hageman, *Pulpit and Table: Some Chapters in the History of Worship in the Reformed Churches* (Richmond: John Knox Press, 1962), 115.
2. James F. White, *The Sacraments in Protestant Faith and Practice* (Nashville: Abingdon Press, 1999), 85.
3. J.-J. von Allmen, *Worship: Its Theology and Practice* (New York: Oxford University Press, 1965), 148.
4. Gordon Lathrop, *What Are the Essentials of Christian Worship?* (Minneapolis: Augsburg Fortress, 1994), 11.
5. Miroslav Volf, "Proclaiming the Lord's Death," *The Christian Century* (March 3, 1999): 253.
6. Newbigin, *Pluralist Society,* 8.
7. Robert L. Short, *The Parables of Peanuts* (New York: Harper & Row, 1968), 247.
8. Gordon Lathrop, "Worship in the Twenty-First Century: Ordo," *Currents in Theology and Mission* 26:4 (August 1999): 294.

9. *The Constitution of The United Presbyterian Church in the United States of America*, Part 2, *Book of Order*, 21.031.

Chapter 6: What Will the Future Bring?

1. Ian G. Barbour, *Religion in an Age of Science* (San Francisco: Harper & Row, 1990).
2. Garrett Green, *Imagining God: Theology and the Religious Imagination* (Grand Rapids: Wm. B. Eerdmans Publishing Co., 1989), esp. 25.
3. Barbara Brown Taylor, "Preaching into the Next Millennium," in *Exilic Preaching: Testimony for Christian Exiles in an Increasingly Hostile Culture,* ed. Erskine Clarke (Harrisburg, Pa.: Trinity Press International, 1998), 92.
4. Thomas S. Kuhn, *The Structure of Scientific Revolutions* (Chicago: University of Chicago Press, 1970).
5. Merold Westphal, "Postmodernism and the Gospel: Onto-theology, Metanarratives, and Perspectivism," *Perspectives: A Journal of Reformed Thought*, vol. 15, no. 4 (April 2000): 7.
6. Jane Vann, *Presbyterian Worship in a Time of Transition: From Modernity to Postmodernity* (Ann Arbor, Mich.: UMI Dissertation Services, 1994), 221. Several ideas in this chapter come from Vann.
7. Robert D. Putnam, *Bowling Alone: The Collapse and Revival of American Community* (New York: Simon & Schuster, 2000).
8. Mark Searle, "Looking to the Future," in *The Changing Face of Jewish and Christian Worship in North America,* ed. Paul F. Bradshaw and Lawrence A. Hoffman (Notre Dame, Ind.: University of Notre Dame Press, 1991), 231.
9. Douglas John Hall, *Journal for Preachers*, Lent, 2000, quoted in *Context: Martin E. Marty on Religion and Culture*, vol. 32, no. 10 (May 15, 2000): 5.
10. William Strauss and Neil Howe, *Generations: The History of America's Future, 1584 to 2069* (New York: William Morrow, 1991).
11. Lauren Winner, "Gen X Revisited," *Christian Century* (November 8, 2000): 1146.
12. Ibid.
13. Ibid., 1148.

Chapter 7: A New Paradigm for Worship

1. There are varying opinions about projecting hymns and songs onto a screen. A screen should not be used if it becomes the focal center of the worship space. The visual center should be font, table, and pulpit. The advantage of projected texts for singing is that the congregation does not have to find a place in the hymnal, hold a heavy book, or sing looking down. A disadvantage is that the sung texts are completely in the control of the leaders of the service. By contrast, the hymnal is the people's book. With it, they have equal access to texts and tunes. (Yet, photocopied hymns from sources outside the

hymnal have the same disadvantage as projected texts.) Another disadvantage of projected texts is that they almost never include any musical notation, which means that the congregation has to pick up the tune by ear. This is not easy to do, and it also puts the congregation entirely at the mercy of the musician(s). Harold M. Best (in *Music Through the Eyes of Faith* [San Francisco: HarperSanFrancisco, 1993]) says that hymnals are important. "And we need to keep reading, both words *and* music. As important as oral tradition is, we also urgently need to keep alive the craft of reading music" (200).

2. "We All Believe in One True God," *Lutheran Book of Worship* (Minneapolis: Augsburg Publishing House; Philadelphia: Board of Publication, 1978), 374; "I Believe in God Almighty," *Sing! A New Creation* (Grand Rapids: Calvin Institute of Christian Worship, 2001), 175.

3. *Book of Common Worship* (Louisville, Ky.: Westminster/John Knox Press, 1993), 471.

4. Malcolm Gladwell, *The Turning Point: How Little Things Can Make a Big Difference* (Boston: Little, Brown & Co., 2000), 77–78.

5. Report from the Milwaukee Symposia for Church Composers, in Frank Burch Brown, *Good Taste, Bad Taste, & Christian Taste: Aesthetics in Religious Life* (New York: Oxford University Press, 2000), 185.

For Further Reading

Barbour, Ian G. *Religion in an Age of Science.* San Francisco: Harper & Row, 1990.

Best, Harold M. *Music Through the Eyes of Faith.* San Francisco: HarperSanFrancisco, 1993.

Bradshaw, Paul F., and Lawrence A. Hoffman, eds. *The Changing Face of Jewish and Christian Worship in North America.* Notre Dame, Ind.: University of Notre Dame Press, 1991.

Brown, Frank Burch. *Good Taste, Bad Taste, and Christian Taste.* Oxford: Oxford University Press, 2000.

Byars, Ronald P. *Christian Worship: Glorifying and Enjoying God.* Louisville, Ky.: Geneva Press, 2000.

Clarke, Erskine, ed. *Exilic Preaching: Testimony for Christian Exiles in an Increasingly Hostile Culture.* Harrisburg, Pa.: Trinity Press International, 1998.

Dawn, Marva. *Reaching Out Without Dumbing Down: A Theology of Worship for the Turn-of-the-Century Culture.* Grand Rapids: Wm. B. Eerdmans Publishing Co., 1995.

Eire, Carlos M. N. *War Against the Idols: The Reformation of Worship from Erasmus to Calvin.* Cambridge: Cambridge University Press, 1986.

Gladwell, Malcolm. *The Turning Point: How Little Things Can Make a Big Difference.* Boston: Little, Brown & Co., 2000.

Green, Garrett. *Imagining God: Theology and the Religious Imagination.* Grand Rapids: Wm. B. Eerdmans Publishing Co., 1989.

Hageman, Howard. *Pulpit and Table: Some Chapters in the History of Worship in the Reformed Churches.* Richmond: John Knox Press, 1962.

Keck, Leander. *The Church Confident.* Nashville: Abingdon Press, 1993.

Kuhn, Thomas S. *The Structure of Scientific Revolutions.* Chicago: University of Chicago Press, 1970.

Lathrop, Gordon. *What Are the Essentials of Christian Worship?* Minneapolis: Augsburg Fortress, 1994.

Lathrop, Gordon. *Holy People: A Liturgical Ecclesiology.* Minneapolis: Fortress Press, 1999.

Lathrop, Gordon. *Holy Things: A Liturgical Theology.* Minneapolis: Fortress Press, 1993.

Miller, Donald E. *Reinventing American Protestantism: Christianity in the New Millennium*. Berkeley, Calif.: University of California Press, 1997.

Newbigin, Lesslie. *The Gospel in a Pluralist Society*. Grand Rapids: Wm. B. Eerdmans Publishing Co., 1989.

Niebuhr, H. Richard. *Christ and Culture*. New York: Harper & Brothers, 1956.

Patterson, Ben. *Serving God: The Grand Essentials of Work & Worship*. Downers Grove, Ill.: InterVarsity Press, 1994.

Pritchard, G. A. *Willow Creek Seeker Services: Evaluating a New Way of Doing Church*. Grand Rapids: Baker Books, 1996.

Putnam, Robert D. *Bowling Alone: The Collapse and Revival of American Community*. New York: Simon & Schuster, 2000.

Strauss, William, and Neil Howe. *Generations: The History of America's Future: 1584 to 2069*. New York: William Morrow, 1991.

Taylor, Barbara Brown. *The Luminous Web: Essays on Science and Religion*. Cambridge: Cowley Publications, 2000.

Vann, Jane. *Presbyterian Worship in a Time of Transition: From Modernity to Postmodernity*. Ann Arbor, Mich.: UMI Dissertation Services, 1994.

von Allmen, J.-J. *Worship: Its Theology and Practice*. New York: Oxford University Press, 1965.

Webber, Robert E. *The Renewal of Sunday Worship*. Nashville: Star Song, 1993.

Westermeyer, Paul. *Te Deum: The Church and Music*. Minneapolis: Fortress Press, 1998.

White, James F. *The Sacraments in Protestant Faith and Practice*. Nashville: Abingdon Press, 1999.